AF430910

Options Trading

*High Income Strategies for Investing,
Understanding the Psychology of Investing ,and How to Day Trade for a
Living.*

By: Branden Turner

Table of Contents

Introduction

Congratulations on downloading *"Options Trading,"* and thank you for doing so.

The world of options trading is growing increasingly chaotic, and downloading this book is the first step you can take towards actually doing something about it. The first step is also always the easiest. However, the information you find in the following chapters is so important to take to heart as they are not concepts that can be put into action immediately. If you file them away for when they are really needed, then when the time comes that you actually use them, you will be glad you did.

To that end, the following chapters will discuss the primary preparedness principals that you will need to consider if you ever hope to really be successful in the investing world. This means you will want to consider the quality of your options—including the potential issues raised by their current value, how they can be best utilized in an emergency case to drive in quick cash, and how to operate with them properly.

With stock selection out of the way, you will then learn everything you need to know about trading in a wide variety of markets including stocks, forex, and commodities (using the options instrument in each market). Rounding out the three primary requirements for successful options trading, you will then learn about crucial risk management principles and what they will mean for you. Finally, you will learn how investing is the quickest way to reach financial freedom.

There are plenty of books on this subject on the market, thanks again for choosing this one! Every effort was made to ensure it is full of as much useful information as possible, so please enjoy!

Chapter 1: Understanding the Stock Market

Let's start this book by taking a look at the dynamics of what we will be the foundation of our discussion: the stock market. When we are talking about swing trading with options, in fact, we implicitly refer to the stock exchange. Therefore, having a clear understanding of what goes on in this market, is the first step to become a successful trader.

Everyone or almost everyone has already heard of the stock exchange or its most popular assets, such as the MIB 30 and other indexes or shares of major global companies.

But few among the non-professionals really know the meaning of these often-technical terms and that they are (wrongly) considered reserved for the most aggressive traders.

In fact, the Exchange is a market accessible to everyone, whether through banking products, such as securities accounts, accumulation plans, or through an online trading platform.

The Stock Market

Contrary to what one might think, the history of the stock exchange is quite old, even though its concept has largely evolved over time. Indeed, the stock exchange made its appearance in the fourteenth century in Brussels, Belgium.

Today, even if the stock market is always a place of exchange, it is first and foremost a large market in which financial securities are exchanged. These financial securities may relate to the shares of large companies, bonds, currencies or even commodities such as gold or oil.

However, in this case, it is not a matter of exchanging physical products or merchandise, but only of securities that represent a certain evolutionary value.

General Operation of the Stock Market

Stocks could, therefore, be defined as a market in which buyers and sellers meet. But, unlike the traditional market, it is not the sellers who decide the price of their securities but the buyers.

It is then the order book that accounts for the prices decided in this way.

Ultimately, the more the securities of a stock market are required by the buyers, the higher the price goes up. On the contrary, when demand is weaker, their price falls.

The stock market on which securities can be traded is also called the "primary market." It is therefore on this market that companies can issue what are called "shares," that are then bought by investors, private individuals or professionals.

Thanks to these purchases of securities, companies can obtain the money necessary to make investments.

But the shares are not the only assets traded on this market since there can also be bonds or financial securities.

Investors' interest is speculative given that they buy a security at a price considered lower than the price that could subsequently reach for a gain or receive what are called "dividends" according to the economic performance of the issuing company of these securities becoming " shareholders."

Thanks to this system of securities and the advent of new technologies, the stock market has strongly developed on an international scale. Today there are almost as many stock exchanges as there are capitalist countries, although in most cases this market is virtual and does not include physical "trading rooms," the latter replaced by complex computer networks.

To better understand the importance of the stock exchange, know that in the single financial center of Milan, billions of euros are exchanged every day.

Trading Times on the Stock Exchange

Maybe you do not know it but trading on the stock exchange offers the possibility of dealing online continuously or 24 hours a day, thanks to the overlapping of the opening hours of the different international stock markets. In fact, the world's big financial centers are eight and their trading hours are listed in three major sessions: the Asian session, the European session, and the North American session.

But we must also consider the legal and solar hours that are not the same depending on the time zone. Let's take a look at the most important time zones for the stock market.

The Asian session

At the beginning of the week, the Asian session is the first one to open. This session includes the stock exchange centers of Japan, China, Australia, New Zealand, and Russia as well as other smaller centers. Asian assets and currency pairs including currencies of these countries are therefore the most volatile in these times. The same applies to economic publications.

The trading hours of the Asian session are as follows:

- Opening hours of the Asian market: at 4 in summer and 3 in winter
- The closing time of the Asian market: at 8 in summer and 7 in winter

The European session

The European session is obviously the most interesting for European investors. It is the second to open after the Asian session and also regroups several major stock exchanges including Italy, France, Germany, Switzerland or the United Kingdom. It should be noted that London's financial center is the largest in the world and more than 30% of financial transactions are carried out in this center every day. Trading volumes are therefore very high during the European session and therefore involve extremely volatile and interesting movements in terms of trading.

The trading hours of the European session are as follows:

- European market opening hours: 12.00 in the summer and 12.00 in the winter
- The closing time of the European market: at 16 in summer and at 17 in winter

The North American session

Finally comes the North American session, which is, therefore, the last to open and close the market cycle. Obviously, this session is also one of the most followed by traders all over the world because it is during this period that US assets are traded. This session includes the financial markets of the United States but also of Canada, Mexico and the countries of South America. It is on the stock market in New York that the volatility is higher at this time of day.

The trading hours of the North American session are as follows:

- Opening time of the North American market: at 17 in summer and at 17 in winter
- The closing time of the North American market: at 21 in summer and at 22 in winter

History and General Knowledge

The Stock Exchange is the market where sellers and buyers can trade values, foreign currencies, services, and goods. The stock exchange thus becomes an important place to put companies in touch, looking for resources to support their production and investors.

Already in the Middle Ages, the scholarship gathered merchants and notaries who dedicated themselves to mercantile and financial activities.

In the twelfth century, Venice became the main Italian square; here were introduced some innovations later adopted by other cities such as the negotiation of the public debt and the turn of the bill.

Bruges, in West Flanders, is the first European city to have a physical place for exchange, where the sale takes place according to new stock exchange rules. The industrial revolution leads to the birth of the modern stock exchange in Italy, following the example of Bruges (Trieste, Rome, Milan, Florence, Naples, Turin, Genoa, Bologna, Palermo, and Venice).

We can distinguish two types of market-based on the services and products exchanged:

> the stock exchange;
> the commodities exchange.

The Stock Exchange is the market in which financial instruments already in circulation are exchanged, such as bonds, shares, futures, warrants, etc.; as a consequence, the stock exchange is a secondary market (in the primary markets, investors buy the goods as soon as they reach the market).

In the commodities exchange, the sale involves goods of different types, placed in appropriate warehouses. Here buyers and sellers can exchange the deposit policies, which guarantee the presence of the goods and the right of withdrawal.

The sale and purchase of outstanding securities are regulated by precise rules; once the system of the on-call auction was over, where the agents exchanged paper documents, the market takes place via an electronic circuit where it is also possible to exchange government bonds and bonds.

Among the main types of shares, we distinguish the ordinary ones, as they assign precise administrative and financial rights to the holder (right to vote in the meetings, to request assembly, liquidation, option, etc.).

Preferred stock (preferred shares) guarantee special property rights to the owners; in the event of dissolution of the company, for example, "privileges" are granted in the distribution of profits (as provided for in the company by-laws).

Savings shares grant ownership rights to assets; however, they exclude administrative rights, including the right to vote.

Poster-gate shares provide for limitations in both administrative and patrimonial rights (generally excluding voting rights).

Limited-voting shares include special restrictions on administrative rights, such as voting limited to certain topics; according to American law, they must guarantee property privileges to the owner.

As previously mentioned, the financial market is structured in financial centers, where various financial services are treated.

The largest financial center is in New York, where the Nyse is located (the New York Stock Exchange all commodities), the Nasdaq (technology stocks), and the Amex (the American Stock Exchange collects many small capitalization companies that sell securities of various kinds).

Other important financial centers include Tokyo and London (the most important in Europe).

Psychological Lessons to Better Understand the Stock Market

Because of the continuous ups and downs that have involved international stock exchanges in recent months, many have begun to ask themselves the fateful question: "Is investing in shares still the best strategy to multiply my savings?"

The financial markets, in general, can be an extraordinary opportunity: not only stocks but also cryptocurrencies or forex can give great satisfaction even if, however, it is necessary to have preparation before going into rash choices.

Let me ask you a question: how much did you study or work to achieve the experience you have in your current job? I imagine we are talking about several years and still thousands of hours of study and practice.

Trading is no different. When trading, you compete on a par with people who do it by profession: you must, therefore, have humility, work, perseverance, intelligence, and method. If you really apply, in a few months you can decide to give up your job because you can earn a lot of money with something that requires commitment and constancy, but without being stressed or having to spend all day on the trading sites.

Getting Your Feet Wet in the Stock Market

Are you looking for safe and profitable investments? Finding solutions of this type is not easy, and you know very well. That's why you decided to take the smartphone, the PC or the tablet to deepen.

In this part of the book, we have decided to provide you with 3 concrete solutions to invest immediately, without making endless queues in the bank and without losing control of what you do.

The strategies that we suggest are ordered according to the risk profile, so we start from the less risky ones to get to the more aggressive ones.

We have written it in several books of this series, we underline it here too for safety: there are no safe investments and at the same time with double-digit returns. The times of government bonds and generous postal coupons have long since come to a close, the current economic situation sees interest at historic lows owing to the ECB's maneuvers in recent years.

In summary:

Few risks = Few Earnings

Many Risks = Potentially Increased Earnings but High Chances for Huge Losses

We come now to the merit of our discussion, here are the best solutions for investing that we have chosen for you.

Santander Consumer Bank is the most remunerative deposit account

Are you looking for a 100% capital guarantee? The deposit account is the best solution even if, in light of the considerations made before, you do not have to expect double-digit returns.

The best deposit account of the moment is that of Santander Consumer Bank which offers you an annual 1.8% on deposits at 36 months.

The advantages of Santander's offer can be summarized as follows:

- 100% security;
- Open it online: no stress, if you are from a PC, you just need to fill out a form (you can do the same thing if you are on a smartphone) and just leave a few data. The procedure will be completed by phone at the time you indicated;
- No penalty in case of early release: if you withdraw money before the scheduled time, you lose nothing;
- 0 Opening costs and management fees: you do not have to pay anything to make money.

To all this, we must add that Santander also provides the unconstrained option that allows you to receive 0.5% per year on free sums. This option can be mixed with the tied one: for example, out of 30 thousand euros, 20 thousand can be tied up at an interest rate of 1.8%, while the remaining 10 thousand free ones receive 0.5%.

Santander is a solid institution, active throughout the world with 122 million customers and over 160 years of history and is now the best solution for those looking for a deposit account free of risks and concerns.

MoneyFarm: the tech alternative to depositing accounts

MoneyFarm is an American start-up that has created a convenient platform to invest online: it is easy to understand and is safe, as we have also explained it in our review.

You can earn up to 5.41%.

The bank deposit accounts, at this stage, have returns that only in a few cases exceed 1.5%. If you're looking for granitic safety, go back to paragraph 1 where we talk about Santander.

However, if you are looking for better profitability at the same risk, you should pay attention to what you are reading. MoneyFarm, in fact, is an alternative to deposit accounts because it offers balanced investments with an almost similar degree of risk.

By signing up for MoneyFarm, you have the following advantages:

- Personal assistance of a team of competent advisors;
- Choose where to invest by filling in the questionnaire in which you indicate your degree of risk;
- You can start testing the goodness of the platform even with a small capital: just $ 500 is enough to try.

With MoneyFarm you can plan your investments and earn up to 5.41% per year, choosing the composition of your portfolio based on your risk profile. MoneyFarm aims to invest in funds with lower operating costs and to guarantee maximum transparency to customers.

You can start investing immediately even at $ 500. Before choosing the strategy, the team of experts helps you to plan your goals exactly.

Registration is free: it takes 3 minutes to start to know it, you can also try it on a smartphone as it is really very easy to use.

Unlike many structured platforms for high-risk investments (think of trading or options), MoneyFarm allows you to operate even if you have a low-risk appetite and is undoubtedly a real alternative to deposit accounts or other banking products that make a lot less.

The portfolios are constantly monitored by a team of experts, and free assistance is guaranteed for the entire duration of the relationship.

It is possible to use the live chat service or to set up a telephone appointment thanks to a special toll-free number. The seriousness is certified by the prizes and awards obtained by leading international financial experts and opinions on the web that are definitely positive. You also choose how much you are willing to risk, and the staff helps you plan the route step by step.

Social Trading

Compared to the previous solution, we are facing a decidedly riskier way: let's underline it immediately, to avoid misunderstandings. If the world of finance interests you, keep reading because you found what you were looking for.

Have you ever tried to approach online trading? If you did and you gave up, most likely you came across the difficulties of a world where only the professional traders, that is, have experience, years of study and time to constantly monitor what is going on. happening in the market in which they operate.

The social trading we want to talk about is precisely created to solve this gap in skills between professional and non-professional investors. eToro, the first social trading platform, allows you to make copy trading: you can, in other words, copy the winning strategies of top traders emulating their successes.

The principle is simple: by investing as the best, you earn like the best.

How does eToro work?

eToro allows its members to copy the strategies of the best American and world traders, called popular investors. Top traders are certified and chosen among the best that invest through the platform.

In particular, you can order them and select the ones that interest you the most according to two criteria:

1. **Earnings** - Simple: see who made the most money in a given period (6 months, 12 months, 24 months) and copy from those who have achieved gains of 25%;

2. **Risks** - If you want to adopt a more conservative strategy, you only need to copy from traders who say they risk less, to limit

your exposure to losses.

With eToro it is possible to invest in the following markets:

- stocks;
- forex;
- criptovalute;
- commodities;
- CFD.

Of course, copying from the best does not completely eliminate the risks because past earnings are not a guarantee for the future. You will agree, however, that when you decide to dedicate yourself to finance, the risk is part of the game, and with social trading, you have the opportunity to take it down in the initial phase and learn from the best.

There are already 4.5 million investors who have relied on social trading to invest like the best: if finance fascinates you and you do not think you have a great experience, eToro is the most effective solution to start investing.

To start, you only need to:

- Create an eToro account;
- Choose the trader to copy from, taking care to select one with a strategy similar to your goals;
- Deciding how much to invest: $ 190 is enough to start copying from the best ones.

eToro is a win-win system designed to share knowledge and earnings and is the best way to debut on the stock market.

Chapter 2: Common Terms to Know Before Investing

Before getting started, it is important to learn the basic terms and how they are used by the experts. In this chapter, you will find a simplified dictionary with the most popular words related to the investing niche.

Stock Market

The stock market is the digital place where the largest number of transactions involving the shares, i.e., the shares of corporate capital, takes place.

In Italy, for example, the stock market is called MTA - Electronic Stock Market - and it should be noted that it does not coincide with the famous "Borsa di Piazza Affari" but represents one of the most important segments.

In fact, at "Piazza Affari," different types of financial instruments are traded, and the market is divided according to the type of contracts traded in:

- MTA, the electronic stock market;
- SEDEX, the segment in which instruments such as covered warrants and certificates are traded;
- MOT, the electronic bond market in which bonds like (except for those convertible into shares), government bonds, Eurobonds and ABS, i.e., securities deriving from the security of loans are traded;
- TAH, after hours, the electronic market in which it is possible to negotiate after the closing of the Exchange, but only for the instruments of the MTA (shares) and the SEDEX (covered warrants and certificates);
- ETFplus, the electronic market in which UCITS units or

shares are traded (SGRs and Sicavs);

- IDEM, the market for derivative instruments (futures and option contracts on currencies, interest rates, and financial instruments). Exceptions are forwarders that are derivative contracts traded on OTC markets, over the counter, that is not regulated.

Market Capitalization

The stock market is also divided into sections by the capitalization threshold.

What, however, is the market capitalization?

The size of a listed company is measured in capitalization, that is, the value given by the number of shares available for that company multiplied by their market price.

The sections in which common markets are divided are:

- Blue chip, where the shares of the 40 largest companies are traded (over 1000 million euros);
- Mid Cap, where the securities of the 60 listed companies with high capitalization are traded but which do not fall among the Blue chips;
- Small Cap, where the shares of companies that do not fall between the Blue chips or the Mid Cap are bought or sold;
- Micro Cap, for companies that do not fall within the minimum liquidity criteria necessary for the other segments;
- Star, for companies with a capitalization of between 40 and 1,000 million euro, but with high transparency, governance and liquidity requirements;
- MTA International where the shares of companies listed on EU exchanges are traded.

Stocks

The stocks are portions in the shared capital of companies, incorporated in joint-stock companies. The two main types of stocks are:

- **Ordinary Stocks** - are those held by the shareholders of a company. They hold voting rights in corporate assemblies and profits deriving from dividends and capital gains;
- **Savings Stocks** - shares of this type do not have voting rights, but they guarantee patrimonial privileges such as dividends, i.e., the distribution of profits. They are mainly intended for small investors.

Stock Value

Each share of each company is traded or bought or sold on a price basis: the market value. This price evolves continuously by the number and the sign of the contracts concluded.

For example, if you read that the Enel stock is up today, it means that many investors are buying Enel shares.

For the classical laws of economic demand and supply, if the demand rises, the price also rises. At the end of the day, when the session is officially closed, the official price of the Enel share will be obtained in this case, by the result of all the fluctuations that the value of the stock suffered during the session based on the number of exchanges it is traded on.

What drives an investor to buy the shares of a company at that particular moment? As we have already said, the formation of share prices is a dynamic process like any other commodity market.

The value of a company stock affects:

- Corporate performance (the state of health of the company, the size of its assets, future growth prospects, ownership structures, extraordinary finance transactions such as acquisitions, mergers and demergers): the improvement in performance is matched by an increase in price and investor's propensity to buy those shares; vice versa, the opposite happens, that is, depreciation. Who owns those shares will sell them, increase the bid and drop the price in question;

- performance of the sector, or the performance at the same time as other companies belonging to the same sector, also on other global stock exchanges;
- macro or foreign policy data directly or indirectly relevant to a company: positive news generate purchases and appreciation, negative news push sales and the depreciation of the stock;
- news or rumors about the company, such as the discovery of new deposits for companies in the oil sector, or the registration of a new patent for a company in the pharmaceutical sector or news about possible mergers, joint ventures or acquisitions.

CFD

This is a key point that actually explains why there is much less bureaucracy for forex trading than for buying and selling bank shares. CFDs (Contract for Difference) are contracts for differences that follow the performance of a given underlying (share, currency, index, etc.) and that can be exchanged, that is, bought or sold. CFDs differ from shares because they are not co-owned by a company and therefore do not give voting rights to those holding them. However, CFDs offer the same economic benefits as equities, such as profits, dividends, and splits.

In even more technical terms, the CFD exchanges the difference in value between the opening price of the certain underlying security (e.g., share) and its closing price. Following this mechanism, the trader who negotiates CFDs:

- Gets a positive result if it buys before the underlying goes up
- Gets a negative result if it sells before the underlying goes down

The mechanism is very simple, and we are sure that it is already clear. We need to buy if we think that a stock is close to the upside, we need to sell it if we think that a stock is close to the downside. CFDs follow the values of the underlying assets so you can get positive results just like shareholders, but playing at home from the comfort of your home.

IPO

A good definition of IPO is that the Initial Public Offering is an instrument governed by the law through which a company obtains the dissemination of its titles among the public. Using what is technically called the creation of the float, the company obtains the listing of its securities on the regulated market.

Said in these terms may seem difficult. For those who are just beginners, we can say that the IPO is a solicitation to invest. Thus, the Initial Public Offering is a real invitation to invest. Having clarified the meaning of IPO let's move on.

How does the Initial Public Offer work? The legislative background of this application is represented by the Consolidated Law on Finance (Legislative Decree 58/1998). This law provides for a whole series of provisions on information and transparency. The indistinct public of the subjects potentially interested in the IPO (recipients of the offer) has the right to know all the useful information to decide whether to join the IPO in full awareness.

The IPO process is decidedly long and complex. By regulation, the IPO foresees the involvement of a series of very different subjects. The following subjects participate in the various phases of the Initial Public Offering:

- the issuing company
- the global coordinator
- the sponsor
- the specialist
- the financial advisor
- the law firms in charge
- the members of the placement consortium

When one wonders how the IPO works, it should be noted that the first phase of the process is represented by the sending to SEC of the prior communication from the company concerned. The prior communication is an official document that the company presents to SEC. The same company that aims to be listed on the stock exchange is responsible for drawing up the Prospectus according to the legal framework.

From what we have said, it is easy to deduce that an IPO can last even a month. If you consider the whole procedure for admission to the stock market, then you also get to 4 or even 6 months. In short, before betting on the performance of a listed, must pass quite a bit of time. The long times, of course, also impact on the possibility of trading CFD on the shares of that listed company.

Bookbuilding an IPO

When referring to this method for fixing the price of the offer on the stock exchange, the first question concerns the definition of bookbuilding. With this strange term, we indicate the process by which the application form of the institutional investors who have submitted an order concerning a security offer transaction is drafted. Through this process, the price of the same securities is set.

The IPO bookbuilding provides for the formation of the price range through the demand expressed by the institutional investors themselves.

The global coordinator manages this process. This figure has the task of collecting all the purchase/subscription orders of institutional investors in a book called the institutional book. Orders are collected based on price or time priority or size. Each order can be expressed in the number of shares or in counter value. Finally, each order is linked to the price limit indicated by the originator. Through this process, it is possible to draw a curve which shows the price of the IPO.

Mutual funds are financial institutes whose purpose is to invest the funds raised by savers. The aim is to create value, through the management of a series of assets, for the fund managers and for the investors who have invested in it.

Three main components characterize a mutual fund (later simply fund):

- The fund's participants are the investors who invest in the fund's assets, acquiring shares through their capital
- The management company, which is the management hub of the fund's activities, which has the function of starting the fund itself, of establishing its own regulation and managing its portfolio
- Depositary banks which physically hold the fund's securities and keep cash in hand. The banks also have a controlling role on the legitimacy of the fund's assets by the provisions of the Bank of America and the fund regulations.

The costs incurred by those who enter into a mutual fund are the following:

- The entry or subscription commission paid at the time of the first payment. It is generally inversely proportional to the size of its investment (the more you invest, the less you pay) and it is higher for the so-called equity funds than for the balanced ones. There are also funds that do not provide for an entry fee:

they are the so-called no-load funds

- The management fee, on the other hand, is the cost borne by the cross-party fund manager. It is calculated on an annual basis but generally paid on a semi-annually, quarterly, or monthly basis.
- The extra-commission of performance is instead an optional commission that some self-financing funds to reward if, thanks to their ability, the fund's return exceeds a certain threshold based on pre-established parameters.

Mutual Funds

The unit value of each individual share of the various funds is published daily in the newspapers. On the NASDAQ website, it is also possible to follow the price trend of the shares of the various funds in exactly the same way that the trend of the shares is followed. The prices in question already incorporate the return on the fund.

There are various types of mutual funds, the best known are the following three:

- Equity funds invest mainly in shares or convertible bonds. They are generally riskier but tend to guarantee higher returns and, in any case, guarantee lower fluctuations than simple equity securities as they generally balance their share with non-equity investments such as ordinary bonds, government securities and with the liquidity held. Another way in which risk balancing is generally achieved is to differentiate by geographical area and therefore also by evaluating the fund's investments.
- Bond funds, these are funds that invest mainly in ordinary bonds and government bonds: this type of funds generally has the advantage of being less risky, but the disadvantage of being less profitable

- Balanced funds are funds that aim to balance the various forms of investment to obtain performance and risk profiles initiated between those of equity and bond funds.

Chapter 3: Stock Market Research and Analysis

Markets in recent times have become more complex, but also more volatile.

In simple words, the risk is increased. Economic factors, central bank interventions, negative rates, low inflation, and algorithms are changing the equity, currency, and commodity markets.

It seems that you no longer look at the fundamentals, but you buy the title of the moment and the one that presents a lower risk (or, to say it better, people think it presents a lower risk). In such difficult markets, small investors who invest in the stock market do not have an easy life. But this does not mean that they have to abandon the shares: with hard work and perseverance, everyone can become a skilled investor.

Fifteen Most Common Mistakes of a Beginner Investor

To help you start your journey, we have collected 15 of the most common mistakes beginner investors make. If you are able to avoid them, you will be one step ahead of the competition and will better understand how to analyze the market.

Relying on Emotions

Most people lose on the stock market because they cannot manage their emotions.

It is proven that small savers buy in the upward phase of the markets, and panic sells at the first sign of decrease. Then what happens is that the market recovers and they are now out.

This happens because of the poor financial education of the average American investor.

One who does not know how to assess the risk does not know the diversification and cannot select the securities to put in the portfolio. He does not know how to calculate the average value of an asset.

He does not even know how to use a spreadsheet to calculate the volatility of a stock.

And it is precisely the lack of ability to manage the risk that will make him make bad decisions and will ultimately result in a loss.

Speculating, not Investing

Another mistake that many often make is to confuse speculating with investing.

If you invest for the very short term, you increase the risk, and it is not a question of investment but of speculation. Knowing how to define investment speculation is essential.

Before entering a title, you must define your time horizon and consider where to put the stop loss. One classical example of speculation is "binary options." They are often promoted as an investment, but they are not. For those who do not know what they are, binary options are bets placed on the price of an asset in the next 30 seconds. Yes, you read that right. Seriously, stay away from them.

Investing Without Planning

On the stock market, invested capital should not be necessary for daily life.

Before investing, plan these goals. Someone invests because in the future he wants to buy a bigger house. Others may invest for when they retire, but also for a holiday.

There are those who do it for their children. The real question is: why are you investing?

Thinking to be Able to Predict the Future

What do Warren Buffet from Omaha and life coach Tony Robbins have in common? Both agree on the big risk that comes when our money is at stake.

During an interview with CNBC, Tony Robbins warned against a big mistake that is committed when it comes to investing for the future, which is, trying to predict the ups and downs of the market.

No one can predict the future, says Robbins, and legendary investors like billionaire Warren Buffett and the founder of the titanic hedge fund Bridgewater Associates, Ray Dalio, tend to agree.

"Your plan for the future cannot be based on trying to time the market because you're going the wrong way."

Instead of buying and selling shares based on how the small change, Robbins suggests thinking long-term.

"You cannot afford to try and time the market. What we must do is study the long-term elements and have a diversification plan that protects when we are wrong."

Buffett is also an important supporter of this type of strategy called "buy and hold," so much so that he wagered that the S & P 500 stock index would surpass hedge funds (which actively change investments). Now, it seems that most likely he will win that bet, which will bring him an extra $ 2 million in prize money.

Robbins also relies on the advice of Dalio, who founded the largest hedge fund in the world, Bridgewater Associates, which has difficulty identifying the right times to get in and out of investments. So, for Robbins, the best idea remains to look long-term, and both he and Buffett suggest that they consider investing in low-cost index funds the best thing to do.

Not Paying Attention to Costs

We have said it in all languages: costs can kill you financially. Investing € 15,000 for 30 years can result in € 106,000 capital if made with an ETF or a low-cost mutual fund, and € 67,000 if it is carried out with a mutual fund that has 2% of TER. See for yourself.

Realistically, saving costs is the only true "free money" that you can get as an investor. Financial products with high commissions are more often than not skylarks, just think of how overestimated Alfa management's idea is.

Changing the Duration of the Investment "on the Go"

It usually works like this: you have chosen a portfolio assuming a certain duration of the investment, then the market "coughs," an instrument within the portfolio loses 5-6%, you read some negative opinions about it, start to shake like a rabbit and eventually sell. This change of time horizon does monstrous damages: typically, it makes you lose about half of the gains. Solution: invest a little at a time and do not think about it anymore.

Not Diversifying

Diversification is useless only if you are able to predict the future and know what the best investment will be. If instead (as a normal human being) you do not have paranormal divinatory skills, you should diversify your portfolio a little. But without exaggerating (more on that later).

Doing Everything Your Broker Says

If the bank, the promoter or the broker push a product, run to check the costs: in 9 out of 10 cases it is the most convenient product for them and, as you can guess, the most expensive for you.

Not Reading Prospectuses and Contracts Well

By law, intermediaries are forced to write everything they do in a "contract" type of document. Often times, they will do it with that legal language that sends you into narcosis already in the second line. But you have to read everything if you do not want bad surprises. Remember that you are responsible for your money and should not put the blame on others.

Buying Unit-Linked (and Index-Linked) Policies

These policies are among the less transparent financial products that can be found, are padded with high commissions in favor of those who sell them. The seller will tell you a lot of nice stories about the capital guarantee. Beyond the fantasies, with a unit-linked (or index-linked) policy, in 90% of cases you will have an expensive product, with severe penalties in case of early disinvestment and, after 10 or 20 years of payments, you will typically be rewarded with a disappointing performance (but, if you can console yourself, you will have made the man who sold it to you very happy).

Buying Bonds From your Bank

Bank bonds usually make less of a BTP of the same maturity, because they bear implicit charges, i.e., costs. Then, they are on average riskier and less liquid. And this is even more true for subordinated bank bonds, whose holders, with the recent entry into force of the bail-in, are likely to be called to put their hands in the portfolio in the event of the issuer's default. Before buying these bonds, study them carefully, compare them with a governmental or supranational title (like BEI, BIS, etc.) and only then decide.

Believing to Get Rich with Online Trading

The colorful world of online trading is teeming with gurus to convince you that you will become rich thanks to their fabulous courses or their financial market forecasting site. Know that succeeding with trading is very difficult: in the vast majority of cases you will end up losing money and time. Learn to save and invest, not to trade.

Listening to Economists, Politicians, and Mass Media

The noise in the ears distracts: eliminate it. So here is, for you and only for you, our personal list of noises that you have to get rid of.

Economists

Think about how little they have put us right in the story: for example, in 2009 they did not recognize the worst crisis since the Great Depression of 1929, in spite of a myriad of signals and, above all, the fact that the recession was already under its way.

Politicians

Except for rare exceptions, the events of any Parliament are lively, full of funny and quarrelsome characters that combine all the colors, going from crisis to immediate solutions, and then plunge again into tragic crises: perfect plots for journalistic-television sagas. Generally, the impact on the financial markets of all this is low. For example, despite the ups and downs of Atalian politics, the spread has continued on its way, indifferent to everything but the ECB. Going on historical facts of weight, think that after the Japanese attack on Pearl Harbor in 1941 (which dragged the US into World War II) the stock index Dow Jones lost only 6% (and in the following 12 months it gained 2,20%).

Mass media

Newspapers, television. They bombard you with a continuous stream of news and data (often superficially explained), which lead you to deviate from your investment path (see point 2). Every day some economic data comes out: sometimes they improve, sometimes they get worse, but in the immediate future they rarely impact on your investments. Just to say, during the last recession in the Eurozone (which began in March 2012 and ended in June 2013), Eurozone stock markets have gained about 13%. So, you focus on a few important things, check your wallet regularly, follow the right source of information, but do not be paranoid about the news.

Wanting to Become Successful Overnight

Do not be the investor who wants immediate success and who loses patience for daily highs and lows. One who wants quick results is certainly an example of how not to invest your savings if you want to succeed.

Successful investing is a bit like taking care of a vegetable garden. Plants grow slowly, the first few years give little fruits, but then start to grow faster. In general, it is foolish to expect significant results in a few weeks, months or even in a few years. Remember that you do not want to get rich fast, you want to get rich for sure.

Not Taking Profits

It may seem strange, but there are lots of investors that never take out their profits. This is detrimental since they never enjoy the money they earned through investing. It is like getting a gym subscription, but never going to the gym: it is useless and does not bring back to the practice.

The most successful investors always take out profits from time to time. Obviously, we are talking about calculated decisions and planned moves. However, the gold nugget here is the fact that if you do not have the money in your bank account, you cannot actually use it. It may sound silly, but it is a fact that most beginners tend to forget.

Chapter 4: How to Pick a Trading Service and a Broker

The use of shares, whether it is to collect dividends or to speculate on their listing, is an increasingly widespread and interesting practice. The risk of loss is always present but depending on the way you buy and sell your shares; this risk can be reduced. If you are wondering how to buy and sell the shares of large listed companies online, here are some explanations that may interest you.

Buy Shares to Become Shareholders

A large part of private individuals and institutions that buy Stocks do so to become shareholders.

It is the simplest use of actions and their main purpose.

In fact, when a company issues its shares, it is possible to buy them directly online.

However, for the already listed shares, to do so it is necessary to go through an intermediary, which can be an online broker or an online bank.

Of course, it is also possible to buy shares directly from sellers who have bought these shares previously, as well as you can re-sell your shares.

Buy and Sell Shares with Online Banks

The easiest way to buy and sell shares is to go through one of the placement products offered by banks and, in particular, by online banks. Thanks to 100% online operation of these banks, you can easily pass your purchase and sale orders directly via the internet without moving.

The advantages of this system are numerous because it is your bank that will take care of executing your orders and then buying and selling your shares. To take advantage of stock market shares through these systems, you must underwrite an Investment Plan in Shares, a securities account or life insurance, which are the main banking products on the stock market.

The only drawback of this method concerns the expenses that may be higher than those that you would have to pay if you bought and sold the shares yourself.

However, bank commissions rarely exceed 4%.

One of the main advantages of bank placement products is that your purchases and sales of shares are supervised by market intermediaries and you can benefit from advice.

Buy and Sell Shares with Online Brokers

Another method is to contact an online mediator. Their operation is almost identical to that of online banks, with the difference that you do not enjoy assistance and advice, but at the same time, the costs are lower because you decide for yourself what actions to buy or sell.

These online brokers also allow trading through stock market shares, without actually having to buy them. To do this, you just need to speculate on the evolution of their value. The tools that allow you to proceed in this way are CFDs.

Ultimately there are several methods to buy and sell shares on the internet. Before deciding on one or other of these solutions, take care to correctly evaluate the commissions involved as well as your level of knowledge on the stock exchange. Depending on these criteria, each of these two methods has different advantages. It is also good to understand the quotation system of an action to be able to speculate on this type of assets.

"How much does the purchase or sale of the shares cost?"

To answer this question, it is essential to define the strategy that will be adapted to buy or sell your shares.

If you own a stock portfolio through the intermediation of a stock market product, each investment in the purchase or sale will have a cost corresponding to the expenses called "brokerage expenses." These expenses can take various forms and involve different costs depending on the share traded (national, European or international market), the amount of the transaction carried out and, obviously, the intermediary. They can be in the form of a fixed or percentage cost on the amount of the transaction. It is therefore very important to carefully choose your stock market offer and your partner by consulting in advance the details of the charges applied to stock market orders.

Things are simpler for online trading and expenses are generally lower. In fact, to be sure, there are no defined brokerage fees for the sale or purchase of shares on the Stock Exchange from a trading platform through CFDs. Obviously, the mediator has a remuneration, however, but in a different and more transparent form: he applies the spread.

The spread corresponds to a small difference between the real quotation of an asset and the quotation of purchase or sale. As a result, when buying shares, the purchase price will be slightly higher than the real price of the asset in question and, in the case of a sale of shares, the selling price will be slightly lower than the real asset price.

Also, in this case, the spreads can vary from one broker to another and, depending on the type of shares you intend to sell or buy, it is interesting to compare the different spreads applied before opening your online account. The spreads can also be fixed and do not vary or be variable and evolve according to the market situation.

"What shares can be bought or sold online?"

For some years now, the offer of mediators in terms of CFDs on shares has been considerably enriched, and it is now possible to access many stocks from the trading platforms made available to the general public.

Of course, you will find European and international stocks. All the stocks proposed by these platforms are part of the large international stock indexes and are therefore particularly popular and volatile and offer many possibilities thanks to a precise strategy based on technical and fundamental data.

Chapter 5: Ways to Trade

The main method for investing in the forex market, therefore, remains the classic forex market. When you operate on the forex market, you are actually buying and selling currencies.

However, over the years, other financial instruments have been introduced to invest in forex and currencies indices on the forex exchange. We are talking about CFD (contract for difference) and binary options. The main feature of these two financial instruments is the following: when you use them to invest in forex, you will not actually own the lots you are investing in.

That said, for those who do not intend to trade online, it could make little sense. Let's try to clarify. Both CFDs and binary options are contracts between investors and brokers. It's not like the classic forex market, where traders buy and sell among themselves. In CFDs and binary options, the asset movement (in this case the buying and selling of currencies) does not take place.

CFDs and binary options are used to speculate on the performance of the value of equity securities. If the trader's forecast is correct, the operation will lead to a profit; vice versa, if the trader's prediction is wrong, the operation will lead to a loss. So, the mode of operation is similar to the stock market: if I invest on the upside, whether I do it with CFDs or actually buy currencies, I only earn money if the value increases.

As we explained in the previous paragraphs, CFDs are also derivative instruments, so they are used to speculate on the performance of asset values. This means that when you buy and sell CFDs, you will never own the asset traded (as opposed to classic forex trading).

Moreover, as with binary options, with CFDs it is possible to trade on:

- Equity securities

- Equity indices
- Forex currencies pairs
- Commodities
- ETF

Leverage plays an important role in CFD trading: through leverage, we can literally multiply the value of our investment. Just to give an example, if you use a lever of 1: 100 and invest € 100, thanks to this lever you can move well € 10,000 (using only your hundred!). All this is made possible thanks to the leverage, which is a sort of "loan" (if we can define it) by the broker, thanks to which you can invest more money than you really have.

But if we talk about eToro, we can't avoid talking about Social Trading. For those who do not know, eToro was the first broker to have introduced Social Trading in CFDs. Thanks to Social trading it is possible to invest by copying (automatically) the operations carried out by the other traders registered on the eToro platform. All you need is a couple of clicks to find the traders to follow, choose the amount to invest, and you're done. In this way, even novice traders can exploit the knowledge and experience of professional traders, copying their operations.

The online trading strategies are based on the study of mathematical and graphic analysis that can suggest the trader the best moment to buy and sell. As we have seen today, it is possible to invest in the stock market thanks to online trading, choosing between trading binary options and trading with the forex market.

Precise right away that there is no suitable trading strategy for all traders, but there are different trading strategies, based on traders and their style of trading. Therefore, it is possible to customize different online trading strategies on the basis of their trading objectives, their intellectual and psychological abilities.

We also recommend using 2 proven techniques not to turn winnings into losses:

stop loss: it establishes a maximum loss that you are willing to suffer;

take profit: you place a dynamic exit level that rises slowly.

Stocks vs. Other Investments

In this historical moment, the search for high returns has become almost spasmodic. Unfortunately, the expansionary policy of central banks has caused the collapse of yields (now virtually 0). Anyone who wants to get a positive return must take risks.

In this context, many are deciding to invest in stocks. What we are wondering with this chapter is whether it is really worth investing in stocks. The answer? It certainly is worth it, but it all depends on the modality of the investment.

This is an investment that can still guarantee very high performance, provided, however, to follow some guidelines.

The first tip is to use only really affordable platforms to invest in stocks. Among the best, we can definitely remember Plus500 or Markets. These platforms are characterized by the fact that they are very easy to use, even for those who have never worked with the actions but, at the same time, guarantee advanced tools, suitable even for the most experienced and needs. At the time of registration, you receive a free bonus that amounts to 7,000 euros for Plus500 and 4,000 euros for Markets. This is additional capital that can be used to operate on the stock markets but cannot be directly withdrawn. If you use the bonus and you get profits, these profits can instead be taken without problems and without constraints.

Both Plus500 and Markets are Trading Contracts for Difference (CFD) trading platforms: this is a particularly flexible and easy-to-understand derivative instrument that guarantees the possibility of obtaining high profits both when markets rise and fall. This is the second condition that makes it worthwhile to invest in stocks: if you buy shares directly, you earn only when the markets go up. And in today's financial conditions, it's an immense gamble. At this time, it is absolutely not convenient to buy shares, the thing that must be done is to subscribe to derivatives (such as CFDs that are very simple) that have underlying actions. Plus500 and Markets are the ideal solutions for investing in stocks and, incidentally, they also allow investing in forex, indices, commodities, bitcoins, etc.

If you want to invest in shares and you want to earn money, the advice is to open an account on Markets or on Plus500.

Leverage — The Huge Advantage of Stock Investing

Through the use of financial leverage (or simply "leverage"), a person has the possibility to buy or sell financial assets for an amount higher than the capital held and, consequently, to benefit from a higher potential return than that deriving from a direct investment in the underlying and, conversely, to expose yourself to the risk of very significant losses.

Let's see how the concept of leverage works starting from a simple case. Let's assume you have $ 100 available to invest Leverage financial in a stock. Let's assume that the gain or loss expectations are equal to 30%: if things go well, we will have $ 130; otherwise, we will have $ 70. This is simple speculation in which we bet on a particular event.

In case we decide to risk more investing, in addition to our $ 100, also another $ 900 borrowed, then the investment would take a different articulation because we use the leverage of 10 to 1 (we invest $ 1000 having a capital initial only of 100). If things go well and the stock goes up 30%, we will receive $ 1300, we return the 900 borrowed with a gain of $ 300 on initial capital of 100. So, we get a 300% profit with a stock that in he gave a 30% return. Obviously, on the $ 900 borrowed, we will have to pay interest, but the general principle remains valid: the leverage allows to increase the possible gains.

Considering the further case of the investment in derivatives. Let's assume we buy a derivative that, within a month, gives the right to buy 100 grams of gold at a price set today of $ 5,000. We could physically buy the gold with an outlay of 5000 $ and keep it waiting for the price to rise and then sell it back. If we decide instead to use derivatives, we should not have $ 5,000, but only the capital needed to buy the derivative. Let's say that a bank sells for 100 $ the derivative that allows us to buy the same 100 grams of gold in a month to $ 5,000. If in a month the gold is worth 5,500, we can buy it and sell it immediately, realizing a gain of 500 $. With the 100 $ of the price of the derivative, we make a profit of $ 400, or 400%, at $ 100.

Without using derivatives and leverage, with the same $500, I could have earned them only against an investment of $5,000, making a profit of 10%.

What are the potentials of its use?

The potential of leveraging is clear. But be careful: the leverage multiplier effect, described with the previous examples, works even if the investment goes wrong. For example, if we decide to invest $ 100 in our possession plus an additional sum of $ 900 borrowed, if the stock depreciated by 30%, we would remain with only $ 700 in hand; having to return the $ 900 borrowed plus interest and considering the $ 100 of our initial investment we would have a loss of over $ 300 on an initial capital of $ 100. As a percentage, the loss would, therefore, be 300% against a reduction in the value of the share of 30%.

Another element to keep in mind is that the different financial levers can be combined: in this way speculation operations are carried out using a "squared lever" with clear reflections on potential potentials.

What may appear to be an interesting tool with positive potential for the investor, on the other hand, presents risks that must, therefore, be taken into due consideration. In fact, if the financial system, as a whole, works with very high leverage and financial institutions lend money to each other to multiply the possible profits, the loss of an individual investor can trigger a domino effect by infecting the entire financial market.

Banks are typically entities that operate with a more or less high degree of leverage: against a certain net capital, the total assets in which the resources are invested is generally much higher. For example, a bank with equity of $ 100 and leverage of 20 manages assets for $ 2,000. A loss of 1% of the assets entails the loss of 20% of the equity capital.

The development of the market for the transfer of credit risk (from financial intermediaries to the market) has meant that the traditional bank model, called "originate-and-hold" ("create and hold:" the bank that provided the loan it remains in the balance sheet until maturity), has been substituted for many operators from the "originate-to-distribute" ("create and distribute:" the intermediary selects the debtors, but then transfers the loan to others, recovering the liquidity and the regulatory capital previously committed or the pure credit risk (credit derivatives), with benefits only on capital requirements), with the effect of a further increase in leverage. The spread of this second bank model is one of the factors that explain the crisis triggered on the sub-prime mortgage market.

Property price inflation has supported the issuance of securitized loans and the exponential growth of the related market, allowing banks to make huge profits and, at the same time, increase leverage. But "the money machine" could not last long and in the end, many banks found themselves without sufficient capital to absorb the losses deriving from the inversion of the real estate market trend, resulting in fact as failed companies.

In the meantime, the example of the banks has spread within the financial system by spreading to all other financial institutions: leverage had prevailed, especially in the United States, generating a huge volume of risky investments that rested on a fraction infinitesimal of equity capital. We are thinking of the issue of so-called "credit default swaps" (derivative instruments used to hedge against the default risk of the debtor). Some insurance companies were heavily exposed to the real estate market, and when the latter collapsed and the value of mortgages fell, they began to lose without having sufficient capital to absorb the losses deriving from the issue of those instruments.

In order not to risk failing and return to sufficient levels of bank capital, capital increases can be used (not an easy task in times of crisis), the reduction of the amount of loans to businesses (granting fewer new loans and not renewal of those already issued) and the disposal of other liquid assets (mostly shares). The result of all this, in the period of the sub-prime crisis, was a credit freeze and a collapse of the stock market. These are the main channels through which the financial crisis has hit the real economy. Credit rationing affected investments and the fall in the stock market (which adds to the decline in house prices) has reduced the value of household wealth and therefore consumption.

We know that a certain level of leverage is physiological to sustain economic growth, even if we have no indication of what the optimal level is. But history teaches us how in an increasingly globalized and interdependent economic-financial system, leverage can be a trigger for speculative bubbles. And it is in these periods that the strongest disconnection between finance and the real economy is generated.

Earning Potential

The stock market gives the false impression that making money on the stock market is just a matter of choosing the right securities, investing quickly, staying glued to a computer screen and spending the day obsessing over what the investment is. But the truth about how to make money on the stock market is another, and you'll find out by reading the following pages.

The secret that reveals how to earn on the Stock Exchange, buying or selling securities and shares, is well explained by the thought of an investor known throughout the world, Benjamin Graham:

"Real money is made not by buying and selling, but by owning the securities, receiving interest and dividends and taking advantage of the increase in their value in the long term."

More simply, the first secret to understanding how to earn on the stock market according to Graham is to focus on long-term investments, keeping a stock for at least 5 years in your investment portfolio.

Including the first fundamental concept of investing in the stock market, we now concretely analyze how to earn by buying stocks.

Investing in the stock market, buying and selling stocks, for many people is a very attractive prospect. However, we are talking about a real investment, accompanied by risk, and it is necessary to understand that it is not easy to earn on the stock market as some want to make believe.

To understand how to do this, we need to be aware of what we are doing and what are the factors that influence the success or failure of our investment.

Many prefer to turn to a financial advisor and leave it to him to follow the market trend, while others more enterprising opt for the choice to invest through CFD or to buy shares through an intermediary.

On the stock exchange, you earn and lose, and the certainty of the result is not always quantifiable. That's why it is essential to know what the mechanisms of gain and loss are on the stock market and, therefore, how to earn on the stock market, as well as knowing how the stock market works.

Investing in the stock market, buying or selling shares, involves investing in one or more of the many companies listed on the stock exchange, both in America and abroad. Companies have an interest in listing on the Stock Exchange to find new financial resources necessary for their production processes. The investor does not invest for the glory or to favor one company over another, but to have a profit and to earn the difference between the purchase price and the selling price.

But how to make money with stock market shares? Every little saver can decide to invest part of his savings in shares, that is fractions of corporate capital traded on the stock exchange.

Assume that today in some shares have a nominal value of 11.00 euros and a market value of 12.50 euros thanks to an appreciation of the stock following a statement by the company's ad on a contract in North Europe.

The investor wants to earn on the stock exchange and decides to buy 10,000 of those shares through an intermediary. The cost of investing in the stock market will be the number of shares for the price per share. In our case, it is 125.000 euro (12.50 * 10.000), to which must be added commission costs for the operation, which vary from intermediary to intermediary.

The following week, the same shares recorded a rise following the positive result of the quarterly report. The price of those share rises to 13.80, a price higher than that to which the investor has paid the shares (12.50).

The investor decides to sell the 10,000 shares bought the previous week. The broker will give the investor the current value of the shares. This will then have to return 138,000 euros (13.80 * 10,000), then withholding the amount of the commission.

And here is explained how to earn on the stock market.

The realized gain is obtained with the difference between the sale value (or € 138,000 - commissions) and the purchase cost of the securities (i.e., € 125,000 + commissions): in our example, we have a profit of € 12,750.00 (137,850- 125,100).

But if the price of the shares fell, however, from 12.50 to 10.00 euros and the investor had decided to sell, then the result would be a loss.

Penny Stocks

There are two things that trading penny stocks are very much known for:

- You can quickly make a big amount of money.
- There is a high probability that you will lose your investment.

These are two opposing extremes that you will be facing. Of course, your objective is to rake in serious profits. Unfortunately, the majority of people who trade penny stocks fail to make any positive return. In fact, they lose their money. But do not be discouraged; because there are still people out there, the well-experienced and real expert traders who double, triple, and continuously grow their money more than you can ever imagine.

Losing trade is normal. Even well-experienced traders make the wrong investment decisions from time to time. However, you must avoid such mistakes as much as possible. Now, to help cut down your future losses, you should be aware of the risks that you will be facing when you trade penny stocks.

The Risks

Small Companies

The majority of the companies in the penny stock market are small companies. In fact, they can be so small that they do not even meet the minimum capitalization requirement. You will find many of these companies on the Pink Sheets. But then again, as discussed in the previous book, do not buy penny stocks from the Pink Sheets. Since they are small companies, it is hard to tell if they are stable enough and if they will even grow. Many small companies also tend to be less professional. Sometimes the executives of a small company see and treat the assets of the company, including the stocks and penny shares, as their own personal belonging.

Start-Up Companies

Many of the companies that issue penny stocks are start-up companies. Therefore, they tend to have a very limited history that you can track. This makes it risky because you would not know for sure if the business is legitimate or if the company is operating a scam.

Less Transparent

Penny stocks do not have stringent requirements. You can always buy them on the Pink Sheets or over the counter (OTC). Remember that the companies on the Pink Sheets are not required to file with the SEC and to meet the minimum capitalization requirements or capital stock of a legitimate company.

Many companies on the Pink Sheets only reveal very limited information about their business, so it is hard to get sufficient and accurate data. Worse, some companies operate a scam.

Bankruptcy

The penny stock market is not only participated by small and start-up companies, but it also has companies that are about to go bankrupt. Unfortunately, these struggling companies will not reveal that they are already about to declare bankruptcy and will even make their stocks to look like an attractive investment. Of course, there is still a probability of making a good amount of profit when you invest in a company that is struggling to survive, especially when the company is able to save itself from bankruptcy and begin to grow successfully. However, the probability of such an ideal scenario to happen is small. Trading penny stocks are already risky enough; you would not want to take more risks.

The reason why you should not invest in a company that is about to go bankrupt is that you will run the risk of losing everything. Once the company declares bankruptcy and does not have sufficient assets to cover all its debts and obligations to its creditors, you will not be able to get your money back.

Low Liquidity

Penny stocks have low liquidity. With low liquidity, they become open to manipulation. A common type of fraudulent scheme is the pump and dump, in which the value of certain penny stocks are pumped up using some fraudulent marketing hype to convince traders to buy them. As its name already implies, the price of certain stocks is pumped up using some promotional or marketing hype. In turn, traders will find the stocks attractive and make an investment. The penny stocks are then dumped on the traders, and their value begins to fall down.

Take note that the pump and dump scheme can be applied even if the company is actually doing well. In fact, when the company is making profits, the pump and dump scheme will be harder to detect. By adding a few dollars on the price of certain stocks that are already increasing, it is almost impossible for traders to determine whether the increased total value is due to legitimate means or merely a result of a pump and dump scheme.

Speculative

Due to so many factors that affect the prices of penny stocks, it can be said that the penny stock market is highly speculative. An important thing in trading penny stocks is first to buy the stocks that truly have a good value. Unfortunately, with the increasing number of scams, hackers, and frauds out there, it becomes difficult to know whether you are really purchasing a good stock or merely a stock whose value is being pumped. Second, even if you get to buy a profitable stock, many active factors can affect its performance in the market. The best stock today may no longer be considered a good stock by tomorrow, depending on the circumstances. Also, granting that the prices of your penny stocks increase, will the buyers still see them attractive and profitable by the time you want to sell them?

These, among many other things, are the risks faced by traders of penny stocks. Consider also the sad fact that most traders fail to make any profit and simply lose their investment.

Do you think you are up for the challenge? If your entrepreneurial spirit is not crushed by these risks, then get ready for the awesome benefits of trading penny stocks.

The Benefits

Trading penny stocks are one of the best investment opportunities that offer wonderful benefits. So, if you honestly think that you can manage the abovementioned risks, then welcome to the world of high profits — a place where you can double, triple, or even multiply your money by more than 20 times in a short period.

Price

Penny stocks are cheap. A single penny stock only costs less than $5. If you have a lot of money to invest, then you can have thousands of stocks from different companies. If you are on a shoestring budget, then this opportunity is also available to you.

High Potential Return

When you trade penny stocks, there is a potential to multiply the value of your stocks many times over. In fact, there is a potential for the prices of your stocks to double within 24 hours or less.

Unlike blue-chip stocks where a 60% increase is considered a big profit already, such is considered normal when you trade penny stocks. And, unlike binary options where you can gain 90% but has a much higher risk, trading penny stocks can make your money grow by more than 500% within a short period. Also, since the penny stock market is mostly composed of small businesses, there is a high probability for the value of their penny stocks to grow, since small businesses have a lot of space for improvements.

High Volume

You can have thousands of penny stocks for a small amount. Having a high volume of penny stocks is good, especially if you get them from a start-up company that is doing well.

Low or Controlled Risk

Penny stocks are inexpensive. You do not have to purchase a lot of penny stocks to earn a decent amount of profit. You can also diversify your stocks to help minimize your losses. And, unlike trading binary options where you will lose your whole wager when you make a wrong investment decision, you can still keep your penny stocks and sell them. If you are patient enough, there is really no such thing as a permanent loss. Considering the volatility of penny stocks, even if the value of your penny stocks decreases, there is a good chance that it will increase after some time.

Chapter 6: When to Buy and Sell

Since this is a guide for beginners and most people that start out decide to begin their investing journey with stocks, we thought it would be interesting to lay out the foundation of the topic. For those who choose to invest in stocks, the objective is undoubtedly that of obtaining the highest possible remuneration from their investment, which is why the choice of securities on which to invest their money is of fundamental importance.

Invest in Stocks

In this regard, there are no universally valid and reliable rules that allow you to obtain good earnings and eliminate risks of losses; otherwise, the number of investors would be much higher.

In other words, the safe stocks to invest in, if they had ever existed in the past, today are officially extinct! However, this does not mean that plans cannot be made to reduce risk while maintaining a high level of profit. Those who choose to invest in shares today are perfectly aware that there are some parameters that experts believe are essential to consider when identifying the shares to be included in an investment portfolio. These parameters are the capitalization of the company, the profitability of equity, the ratio between profit and price, the ratio of Ratio to price book value, the dividend yield and the ratings/target price. Let's see what these individual parameters consist of in detail, and how we can use them to choose the stocks to invest in today.

Capitalization of Companies

Although this is a very often underestimated parameter, we must nevertheless consider that the size of the company is very often a sign of market power, in most cases through the possession of brands or technologies exploited globally. The use of this parameter, however, makes sense especially for equity investments in the US market, where over the last year companies with high capitalization (Apple, Coca Cola, Facebook, Google, Amazon, etc.) have seen a significant performance. The close relationship existing in the US shareholding between the level of capitalization on the stock exchange and the performance of the stock is one of the factors underlying the growing weight that American stocks have in the portfolios of international investors. The interest of traders in US stocks has also increased in light of the boom in listed companies operating in the tech and web segment.

Return over Equity (RoE)

This is the ratio between the net result and the net assets of a given company. In particular, from the point of view of equity investments is an important parameter as profitability higher than the cost of capital is an index of the ability of an enterprise to create value. From this point of view, the Roe is always held in strong consideration by those who choose to invest in shares today.

Price/Earnings Ratio

A low ratio of this parameter makes a share price particularly attractive, but at the same time, it could mean that expectations regarding future profits are not particularly positive. As in the case of the Roe, this is a factor to be taken into consideration when choosing the best stocks to invest in.

Price/Value Ratio

The ratio between the share price and the net asset value resulting from the last balance sheet, especially if this ratio is lower than the unit means that the company is being paid less than the value of the budget net of liabilities. However, this does not necessarily mean that it is a good deal, since the company may not be able to produce profits either.

Dividend Yield

This is the percentage ratio between the last distributed dividend and the share price. In particular, it measures the remuneration provided by the company to shareholders in the last year in the form of liquidity. This parameter is often taken into account to identify the stocks to invest in since a company is able to distribute dividends is generally a healthy company. But also, in this case, as with all the other selection parameters, it is necessary to make a broader and more complete analysis since a high level of this indicator could also mean that the company has made few investments or has little prospect of growth. For this reason, looking at the dividend yield as a primary factor in determining the securities on which to invest in the stock market is reductive. The dividend yield only makes sense if accompanied by considerations on any business plans and industrial plans of the listed company. Only in this way is it possible to have guarantees on what are the prospects of the group in the future.

Rating and Target Price

The rating is the judgment that certain analysts and investment banks have on specifically listed security while the target price represents the maximum target price to which the shares may reach. Dozens of judgments are published daily on all listed shares. Giving an eye to these judgments is a way to have further clarification on what may be the prospects of the listed. If, in fact, more brokers decide to cut the rating on an X stock from buy to neutral or worse sell, then it means that, indeed, the expectations of the security in question are certainly not positive and therefore, perhaps, it is not the case to insert this title in the list of shares to invest in.

Clearly, promotions and failures (upgrades and downgrades) are not in the air but are accompanied by reports within which are explained the reasons behind that single judgment. Therefore, rating and target price are one of the most important factors for choosing the best stocks to invest in. As the great traders who focus on equities perfectly know, by looking at the history or the evolution of the rating and target price of a single stock, one can have an even more complete picture in the choice of actions to invest in today.

These are the main indicators that will dictate whether your investment will be successful or not. Taking time to study the structure of the company you want to invest in is extremely important since it gives you the opportunity to get a better idea of where it is going and what it is aiming at for the future. Remember that when you invest in stocks, you own part of that project: it is your duty to understand it fully.

Here are some terms that you should familiarize with if you want to get better at stock investing.

One who wants to invest or play on the stock exchange cannot consider or know some terms which are basic for their trading actions. Some precautions must be taken into consideration:

- read constantly and daily, newspapers of an economic nature; this will mainly serve those who are not very familiar with the terminology used and consequently do not know the meaning of Actions, Bots, BTPs, Dow Jones, Nasdaq, Nikkei, etc.
- Watch economic news regularly, in such a way as to familiarize yourself and learn how to pronounce the most used terms;
- Document yourself through books, forums, and online sites. This will greatly facilitate understanding and will also serve as personal cultural baggage. In this way, you can increase your knowledge and take your first steps in the world of economics.

A first term to know is certainly the word *share*, which is the cardinal element of the companies, which represents in all respects a share of the social capital of a company. The shares can be divided mainly into 3 categories:

- **Ordinary Shares**: according to which the holder can express his right to vote;
- **Savings Shares**: there is no possibility to cast a vote but give a greater dividend than previous shares;
- **Preference Shares**: guarantee "a greater privilege" in the allocation of profits and voting power in extraordinary shareholders' meetings.

Chapter 7: Long-Term Investing vs. Day Trading

Very often the concepts of saving and investing are confused, as well as that of "saver" and "trader." However, there are substantial differences that need to be understood, before diving deeper into the subject of money.

In this second chapter, we will explain what saving and investing are, analyzing which choice is more convenient today.

Saving means taking out a portion of income received, that you deliberately choose not to consume immediately, but to store in a bank account for the future. Saving often results in the tranquillity guaranteed by the availability of resources to deal with unexpected situations.

Savings can then be allocated to investment, and this is the main analogy between the two concepts. The investment may be of the "economic" type (such as the purchase of a car or company machinery), or of the "financial" type (such as the purchase of a security or mutual fund with the objective to see capital growth over time). However, unlike savings, in the case of investing, the achievement of the desired objective is not certain (for example, a stock may lose value) so the result can be negative, compromising the amounts saved.

"Which is better?"

If the question that arises is whether it is better to save or invest, the answer is probably "both." The choice depends on your financial situation and your personal goals.

Savings can be used to invest, but it can also be used in other ways. In fact, the money saved can also be deposited in the bank to reduce risks (theft). But this, unlike what many thinks, is a wrong and unprofitable choice: money, in fact, tends to lose purchasing power over time due to inflation. In other words, if you save 100 Dollars today, in 20 years, you will be able to get less out of that money than today. This is why saving money is, often, the wrong choice if you want to get wealthy.

Assuming an average increase in the cost of living around 2% and a saved sum of 5,000 Dollars, in five years this sum will fall to real 4,500 Dollars, that is 10% less (excluding banking taxes!). Obviously, you can keep the savings at home (under the classic mattress!), But with all the risks that come with it.

"What is the difference between trading and saving?"

Let's repeat it once again to get it better. Saving means to put money aside little by little to accumulate a certain sum. Usually, you save for a certain goal, like going on vacation, buying a car or for emergencies that could happen.

Instead, trading means taking a part of the money to make it grow, buying tools that can increase its value like currencies, real estates and ETF's.

"Who should save?"

Obviously, everyone should try to save a part of their money. The rule is to have away on your bank account at least the necessary to "survive" for three months and cover the main expenses (such as food and rent). This will offer air pocket, in case of inconvenient and unexpected situations.

Saving is, therefore, a rule and as every good rule has its exceptions. You can, in fact, stop putting aside the money when:

- you have too much debt, and you are trying to pay it off;
- the family has priority and could not go on in case of unfortunate events to one of its members.

Even when you have set aside enough for emergencies, you do not have to stop saving. The goal of everyone should be to put aside at least 10% of their salary every month, perhaps starting from 5% and gradually scaling up. To make things easier, you can save money by thinking of any objective; like having enough money for a great honeymoon or to get a new car.

Having a goal is essential, so you know what you're saving for. Every reach person has financial goals, so it is a good habit to pick up.

"When is the time to trade?"

Like when you save money, you need to have a goal to when and how to trade your savings. In this case, it is important to know what your short, medium and long-term goals are.

- With "short term" we mean goals for the next 3 years;
- With "medium term," things are planned for the next 3-10 years
- The "long-term" goals are those for which you will not need the money back for at least 10 years or more

For short-term objectives, you usually invest through deposit accounts, which allow you to get a minimum return in a short amount of time. However, this has been a bit shrinking in the last period (deposit rates are at the lowest). For the medium-long term objectives, it is instead advisable to invest in the market, to avoid the reduction in value that inflation produces on "still" money. The market usually guarantees higher returns than deposit accounts over longer periods and having a well-constructed portfolio helps a lot in this regard.

For those approaching or exceeding 30 years of age, having a medium-long term goal is advisable. Investing and setting aside money for retirement can be a good start.

To sum up the concept, everything depends on your time horizon:

- If you think about using the money within one or three years, save it.
- If you do not need this money for the next 10 years, invest it.

If, on the other hand, you plan on using the savings in the next 5 or 10 years, but you want to still have money set aside in your bank account, then you will have to do both. Keep in mind that this is much harder and requires more discipline. However, with the right mindset, it is certainly the best option.

"What does trading wisely mean?"

Since the importance of the investment is well established, it should also be emphasized that there is no recipe to guarantee the success of an investment.

However, following some prudential rules can help minimize risks.

First of all, we need to avoid the dream of making money overnight. On the market, there are professional operators, experts, who dedicate all their time to this activity, but they often make mistakes as well. Just to say how difficult it is and how "get rich quick schemes" do not exist.

One strategy that every investor needs to master to reduce the risk is diversification. This means not putting all your eggs in one basket but, rather, spreading your resources on different assets. When the invested amount grows it becomes more important to diversify not only between the asset classes (stocks, bonds, commodities) but also geographically (considering the currency variable) and size-wise (small or big cap companies to stay within the equity, more or less long maturities for government securities, bonds with different level of risk in the corporate sphere).

Making these choices takes time, that needs to be subtracted from work or other activities. So, in the end, it is about investing time, before moving the money. But it is worth it and, frankly speaking, the only option to avoid reckless choices that you may regret afterward.

Chapter 8: Predicting the Market

Indicators and charts are one of the most important components when we talk about technical analysis. In addition to experience, coldness, and psychology, a good analyst cannot disregard a thorough knowledge of the graphs. The latter can represent different information and may appear in different forms.

In graphical analysis, the graphs deserve particular attention because they represent the price dynamics of a given financial instrument and in a given period.

In the technical analysis, the most commonly used type of graph is certainly the candlestick chart, better known under the name of a Japanese candlestick chart. Before moving on to a detailed description of the candlestick chart, however, I would like to say a few words about two other charts, less used than candlestick charts, but which may be useful as they can help you understand the Japanese candlestick chart.

The price chart is shown on a Cartesian plane where, on the abscissa axis, that is the vertical axis the time is reported, while on the horizontal axis the price is reported.

Given this premise, we can still say that the graphs refer to different time periods whether they are fractions of minutes, hours and days, if not even weeks, months or even years indicating different sizes of opening or closing, of maximums and minima.

On the axis of the abscissas, we find a space called histogram of the volume, which represents the number of instruments exchanged during the period under examination.

In graphic analysis, in the specific and more generally in the technical analysis, various types of graph are used.

Features of a Good Chart

With the above, I do not mean that you will need a chart that contains a myriad of information or detailed information in detail, but I would like to emphasize that the best successful traders on the market, use very few indicators. Yes, you understood correctly. only a few indicators. You will, therefore, think that what has been described up to now is only a chat, but it is not so, as these extrapolate the most important information directly from the graph. The charts obviously can only be provided by the brokers, which as for the forex market, here too we advise you always to choose the best binary options brokers. So, it is not true that the graphics are all the same, it will be a good broker who will extrapolate all the information that interests him from the various detailed charts. And from here, we recognize the best brokers.

The reason for this extrapolation is very simple: since the indicators express only the past in a graphic form, they can provide a very approximate vision of the future. So too many indicators in a chart can sometimes create confusion instead of aid.

Therefore, we consider it very important to keep the following points in mind:

- **Good graphics program** - With this, in fact, you should always be able to look far enough in the past, to plan the future and identify relevant barriers and gather a satisfactory overview. In the binary options charts of the different brokers, this time frame is too narrow to draw reliable conclusions.
- **Good quality graphs always indicate different time intervals.** These range from a few minutes to a max. of a month.
- **Never set just a common linear chart.** This fact would not be very useful for technical analysis purposes. On the other hand, candle or beam charts are used, which we will explain briefly.

"What is chart analysis?"

The analysis of the graphs is above all the search for particular shapes, also called graphic structures, configurations, figures.

They are figures that emerge from the price movement, and that can signal its future trend. They are tracked by analysts joining points in the price graph of financial security or the performance of an indicator.

The purpose of the graphic analysis will, therefore, be to identify the most typical price patterns for forecasting purposes.

These graphic formations can be classified into different categories. The main categories of classes can assume inversion or continuation or consolidation characteristics. The fundamental feature will also be the dynamics of the volumes, which we will explain under each figure.

This is why it takes technique, experience, strategies, if not the analyst's ability to see these forms in the movement of a graph. These are the fundamental elements of this type of analysis. The concept of the trendline, support, and resistance are also part of this aspect of technical analysis.

Most Used Graphs for Graphic Analysis

Below we will list the most used graphs for graphic analysis and explain the operation. Before doing this, however, we must explain another very important and used concept: the figure of Continuation. These have common characteristics in all the graphs, they represent a pause in the prevailing trend in progress and are a prelude to a continuation of the trend in the direction of the direction previously underway. For this reason, they are also known as consolidation figures.

The main difference between the continuation and the inversion figures concerns the extension.

The continuation figures are often accompanied by a decrease in the volumes traded.

One of the first figures we are going to examine is the wedge.

Wedge

This too is a continuation figure on explained and is very similar to the triangle for 2 reasons:

- for the form;
- for the time it takes to form. This differs from the triangle that we will see below because the shape that forms is characterized by a strongly bullish or bearish inclination opposite to that of the current trend.

This means that:

- this chart consists of two convergent trendlines and takes about one to three months to develop;
- in an uptrend, a falling wedge or "a descending wedge" can be encountered; while in a bearish tendency, a rising wedge or "an ascending wedge" can develop.

As with the pennant and flag figures, the wedge can be found in the middle of a movement, thus allowing to calculate minimum targets.

The dynamics of the volumes see a decrease in the course of the formation of the pattern, and it should go to be reduced for all the period of formation of the figure. On the contrary, they increase significantly when the trendline is broken, which is a typical feature of the wedge.

The second figure we examine in this chapter is the pennant.

Pennant

This figure is also quite common in chart analysis.

This figure together with the figure of the flag, which we will see immediately after the flag appears after an almost vertical movement and represents a pause in the trend.

Its characteristic is that it is presented as a symmetrical triangle which, however, has a maximum extension of 3 weeks. Most often, in bearish actions, the refinement time of the figure is even lower and is equal to one or maximum two weeks. The pennant is halfway to the bullish or bearish movement, with the obvious implications in calculating the minimum targets for the movement's arrival.

It will, therefore, be obvious that the volume decreases during the formation of the figure and should be low throughout the formation of the pattern. On the contrary, instead, they significantly increase when the trendline breaks, which identifies the pennant. These are accompanied by a similar trend in the range within which prices move.

Pennants most often coincide with a contraction phase, which does not necessarily have an opposite inclination with respect to the basic trend.

Both this figure and the next develop within a rather short time frame.

The third figure that we examine as announced is the Flag.

Flag

Flag formation, or flag, is a very common pattern of continuation in the graphic analysis. This form tends to appear close to the temporary exhaustion of a trend, which represents a brief pause in the market after strongly accentuated movements, are almost vertical and known as the flagpole.

The flag has a shape similar to a parallelepiped, almost to represent a rectangle, bounded by two parallel trendlines but opposed to the prevailing trend; in other words, it can be seen as a flag that is tilted downward in an uptrend and upward in a bearish trend.

His training ends within a medium period, that is between one and three weeks. It usually appears halfway to complete the movement.

It must also be said that if it is in a bearish movement the perfection time is less and the figure is usually completed in one or two weeks. Precisely because it is in the middle of the bullish or bearish movement, the figure is important for identifying price targets. From here we will then calculate the width of the movement preceding the flag and report this distance after the break of the trendline delineating the figure.

The volume should also decrease during the formation of the figure and then increase again when the trendline is broken.

So, let's see how to use Flag and Pennant.

The targets that can be identified in relation to these figures are two:

- The first is determined by projecting the width of the base from the breakout point; here this target assumes less importance if we consider the reduced dimensions of the figure.
- The second can instead be obtained by projecting, from the breakout point, a distance equivalent to that covered by the movement that preceded the formation of the pennant.
- This means that these figures often materialize around half of the overall movement, giving a fair advantage at the operational level.

The temporary phase of price weakness can be exploited to enter the stock or even just to increase the position taken earlier, again using a stop-loss much lower than the potential take-profit.

The fourth figure that we will explain will be represented by the rectangle.

Rectangle

The rectangle is the simplest among the figures proposed by the technical analysis.

It identifies a phase of price congestion. In Technical Analysis, with this term, we mean a graphic formation in correspondence with which prices oscillate within a narrow range of values. This process takes place when the market moves sideways.

The pattern represents a break zone of the current trend in which prices move sideways. This also gives rise to the name of the trading range or congestion area, a figure that represents a period of consolidation of the current trend that is resolved in the direction of the trend that preceded it. This represents a fundamental figure, to correctly identify the continuation pattern if not also the observation of the volumes.

Also, for this bullish figure, the rebounds must be accompanied by high volumes, with the corrections characterized by decreasing volumes. In the opposite case, instead, in the bearish rectangle, are the corrections to have more accentuated volumes.

Many investors, take advantage of the oscillations, selling to the top of the figure and buying at the minimum. However, those who use this approach risk not exploiting the breaking of the pattern.

The figure in question usually takes from one to three months to improve, and the minimum target is represented by the translation of the height of the rectangle when the price breaks the figure.

Prices move within a fixed band identified by support and resistance as better shown in the figure below.

first target 1

The rectangles can also be configured as inversion figures, depending on the context in which they are formed. It is therefore evident how the congestion phases identify a moment in which the market expresses considerable uncertainty and awaits new information to decide the future trend. Unlike the contraction phases (in which the continuous reduction in volatility identifies in an increasingly precise manner the moment in which the market will receive the information that awaits) a figure of congestion like the rectangle does not allow to identify sufficiently in advance the moment in which the breakout will take place.

The operational cues that this figure can provide are basically of two types:

- The first requires waiting for the exit of prices from the congestion zone initially identified. This exit must necessarily be classified as a breakout and therefore must be characterized by an increase in volumes and volatility.
- The second operational step derives from the possibility of exploiting the lateral movement of prices to buy close to the identified support and sell when the values are near the top of the figure again.

Support and Resistance

Let me now explain briefly what the supports and the resistances are.

Support is defined as that price level at which there is, an arrest of the downward trend in prices. An excessive concentration of purchases that occurs in the vicinity of the same will cause a block in the downward trend in prices.

A level of support is defined as reliable when it shows resistance to repeated "attacks" without a bearish breakdown.

The Resistance is defined instead as that level of price where the growth of the same stops. In the case of the Resistance, the high concentration of sales prevents the continuation of the increase. A resistance level, on the contrary, is stronger and more reliable as it resists repeated "attacks" without an upward failure. Surely, a historical minimum or maximum represents a level of Support or Strategic Resistance.

Consequently, the penetration or breaking of support levels or even resistance can be caused by:

- important changes in the fundamental values of a company (increase in profits, changes in management, etc.);
- from simple forecasts based on price trends in recent times;
- both levels of support and resistance can also arise from motivations exclusively of an emotional nature. Supports and resistances represent with great simplicity the encounter/clash between supply and demand.

From the above it is clear that in practice, a breakout, or an event in which the price comes out of a trend, breaking a support or resistance or a channel, above a level of resistance evidence an increase in demand, arising from more buyers, who are willing to buy at higher prices than the current ones.

In the opposite case, instead, the breakdown of support shows an increase in the sellers, and therefore in the offer, as more sellers are willing to sell even at lower prices than the current ones.

If a level of support is broken, it automatically turns into a resistance level, just as if a resistance level is broken, it becomes a level of support. This process is known as a pullback, which is a time when a trending market takes a break.

The support and resistance lines can be drawn horizontally and then we will talk about static support, where the support corresponds to a precise and constant point in time; both obliquely and in this case, we will talk about dynamic support, where a trendline is drawn with the variation of prices and with the passage of time.

The fifth figure concerns the triangle.

Triangle

In technical analysis, that of the triangle is a consolidation figure and is used to verify the continuation of the main trend. This is a pattern that lasts a few months when there is a pause in the current trend with prices that oscillate in an increasingly narrow area.

The figure has the following characteristics:

- The triangle must have a minimum of four reaction points; two superiors, and two inferiors; the first ones necessary to trace the upper trendline, the seconds necessary to draw the lower trend line.
- The triangle is characterized by a time limit for its resolution. Usually, the prices break the triangle at a point between two thirds and three-quarters of the depth of the triangle.
- The volumes in the formation phase of the triangle waves lose strength and then explode when the trendline that delimits the figure breaks.
- The minimum target for price trends is calculated by projecting the maximum height of the triangle.

The figure in question can present itself according to three different structures:

Symmetrical Triangle

The Symmetrical Triangle has the trendlines that delimit it that are convergent.

Prices tend to move in a range that gradually becomes narrower with the passing of the sessions, due to a constant reduction of the maximums, and also due to a constant reduction of the minimums.

Descending Triangle (characterized by a flat demarcation line, the lower one, and by a bearish trend line, the upper one.)

In this figure, there will be a greater conviction on the part of the bearish and is often found during a downward trend.

The reduction in the range within which prices move, occurs only thanks to an increase in the minimum, while the maximums remain almost unchanged.

Just such behavior makes evident the greater pressure of the buyers with respect to the sellers and attributes to this figure a bullish value.

Descending triangle

The figure represents a symmetrical structure, which makes it difficult to interpret. In the third case, on the other hand, we speak of an ascending triangle, characterized by an upper line of flat demarcation and a line, the lower, ascending line. This pattern indicates a greater strength of the uptrend and is often found during an uptrend

Regardless of the configuration, whether symmetrical, ascending or descending, it is possible to calculate the target of the figure, i.e., the level that prices should reach in the phase following the breakout.

This is calculated by projecting, from the breaking point, the "base" of the triangle, i.e., the maximum width that the figure recorded during its formation.

The sixth figure in question concerns the formation of broadening.

Broadening

This represents a rather rare figure, classified as a variant of the triangle but which presents a contrary opening, with divergent trendlines. It is a figure that occurs at the end of a trend, usually bullish.

The dynamics of the volumes are different from that of the triangles, as the volume gradually expands together with the increase in price oscillation.

The seventh figure that we are going to examine concerns the diamond.

Diamond

Also, the diamond as an inversion figure is one of the rarest and one of the least simple to detect. Graphically the diamond is formed by a double-figure composed of a first half that recalls the shape of a broadening from a second half that resembles a symmetrical triangle.

A diamond can present itself in two circumstances:

- at the end of an uptrend;
- at the end of a bearish trend;

In the first case, it takes the name of "Diamond Top," and vice versa, we would be facing a "Diamond Bottom."

The figure does not always develop symmetrically. Often, the second half is prolonged in time more than the first one did.

By its nature, the diamond needs very dynamic market phases. The figure of the Diamond can also occur during simple breaks of the trend.

For this reason, it is easier to find the diamond at the peak of an upward trend before a bearish reversal rather than the other way around. The dynamics of volumes go hand in hand with that of prices. That is, if volumes increase, prices increase. In the second half, however, prices fall and consequently also volumes.

There are 4 basic elements to identify the training:

- an initial phase of price expansion;
- a maximum;
- a minimum;
- a phase of price contraction;

The pattern is only complete when the support or resistance line breaks and a pullback to the violated trendline do not always occur.

The minimum price target is equal to the maximum vertical distance between the two extreme parts of the figure projected at the bottom (or at the top) with respect to the breaking point of the support or resistance. It is possible, even for the diamond, to calculate a target price.

It is sufficient to project the maximum width of the figure and project it from the point where the breakout occurred.

If it is configured as a continuation figure, it is also possible to derive a second target, projecting the width of the movement that preceded the beginning of the diamond, from the point of the final breakout. diamond breaking points

The eighth figure we examine will be a figure difficult enough to examine and represents the rounding and spike.

Rounding and Spike

This represents one of the many figures of inversions, which presents itself as a slow and gradual movement on the lows that will first have a slight downward, then lateral and then shows a growing movement.

The pattern is one of the slowest of all the graphic analysis and is usually identifiable on longer-term charts.

It is really difficult to establish the precise moment in which the figure can be considered complete, if not after the first substantial rises. More difficult, it will be to identify upward targets.

Spike is also very special. The figures in question show, without any transition period, a sudden reversal of the quotations. An inversion accompanied by an explosion of volumes.

Due to its characteristics, the figure in question is difficult to identify in advance.

Double Top and Double Bottom

Also, this falls into the categories of the inversion figures, which we remember are particular graphic figures that announce an inversion of the current trend. The figure in question turns out to be a very common figure in graphic analysis and together with other figures, the double bottom and double top figures are among the most common and recognizable formations.

We explain briefly in two essential steps, its operation;

1. **The double minimum is at the peak of a bearish trend and is configured as a minimum, a subsequent rebound and a subsequent fallback to the level of the previous minimum.** The ascent that follows leads to the completion of the figure. The pattern, due to its shape, is also called a formation in W. Volumes are growing during the formation of the first minimum, down in the following rebound, and then increase again during the upward movement that completes the figure.

Basically, therefore, the double minimum is realized, following a clear bearish trend, in which prices test twice a price threshold, but without being able to overcome it. This determines the realization of two minimums slightly spaced over time. Double minimum and double maximum.

1. Also, **the characteristics of the double maximum are the same, but the pattern has a secularly opposite**

development. The double top is at the height of an uptrend and is configured as a maximum, a consequent fall and a subsequent rebound towards the previous maximum.

The double maximum is achieved when, following a sharp uptrend, prices test twice a price threshold, but without being able to overcome it, determining the formation of two maximums. Volumes are growing at the formation of the first rise, remaining lower in the formation of the second maximum and then increasing conspicuously at the time of the piercing of the traceable line starting from the previous minimum.

In both figures, it is possible to observe a return of prices to the level of completion of the pattern, in a pullback similar to that of the head and shoulders that we will see later, before the definitive start of the new trend, bullish in the double minimum and bearish in the double maximum. This pullback is accompanied by small volumes.

The measurement of the minimum upward (or downward) target is calculated by calculating the distance between the line joining the two minima (or the two maxima) and the first maximum (or minimum) relative and projecting this value from the upward drilling point or downward.

in essence, the double minimum or the double maximum is, however, a graphic formation with a degree of reliability lower than other figures of inversion, both because it is not always detectable with sufficient certainty, and because it often occurs in conditions of volatility so high that allow identification of a valid breakout.

Triple Top and Triple Bottom

The triple maximum and the triple minimum are also inversion figures, defined as variants of the head and shoulders, but unlike the previous ones, the three maxima and the three minima are all placed at the same height.

The volumes to be considered, in the triple minimum correspond to each rise, starting from a minimum is accompanied by decreasing volumes. The pattern is completed when the line obtained by joining the last maximum with extremely high volumes is breached upwards. triple maximum

In the triple maximum, any downward correction starting from a maximum is accompanied by declining volumes, and consequently, the figure can be said to be complete, when the level obtained by joining the last lows is violated downwards with volumes in great growth. In the triple minimum, however, the minimum target is common to that used for head and shoulders (a figure that we will see shortly), if not also equal to the double minimum and double maximum, based on the height of the figure.

Chapter 9: Diversification and Managing Your Portfolio

How to diversify your investments? A good question that all investors ask themselves. After all, we must start from another question: why is it important to diversify your investments? Simple: to reduce risks. It goes without saying that investing in several different assets involves a better distribution of risk. So, if, for example, an action is at a loss, we will always have the hope that precious metal is on the rise instead.

Below we will try to offer a comprehensive picture on how to diversify your investments, thus better understanding why it is important to diversify your investments.

Why is it important to diversify? We have said that this practice is useful for reducing investment risks. The world today is globalized, so even the stock exchanges are extremely connected to each other. Therefore, the crisis of an exchange carries with it all the others. Furthermore, today's World, especially since the 1990s with the collapse of the Berlin Wall, has become economically very variable and unpredictable. The logic that drives diversification responds to the impossibility of knowing in advance the future performance of our investments. A variable in which, substantially, the risk of each investment lies. The basic idea to minimize the risks deriving from this uncertainty consists in splitting its investments into different projects, thus spreading the risk linked to the performance of individual investments.

Moreover, each asset is linked to multiple variables. For example, actions are closely related to a company's performance. Which, often, also hides its real financial situation. Or agricultural raw materials, just a bacterium that destroys the crop to cause a collapse. Regarding the extraction of oil, just the disaster of a platform or a strike of the workers to cause the collapse of the flock. And what about a coup or unexpected election results.

How to diversify your investments? Before finding an answer, it is necessary to understand that investments are divided into 5 large areas:

- **Stock** - Area consisting of all shares, funds, ETFs, individual securities
- **Real estate** - This area includes financial instruments related to real estate
- **Commodities** - For commodities, we mean all those products mainly related to the soil, then cultivable. Like coffee, cocoa, sugar, soy, wheat. But also, to the subsoil, like the energy fields like oil, gas and so on.
- **Precious metals** - Precious metals include, as you can guess, gold, silver, platinum.
- **Bonds** - Bonds include both government securities and bonds issued by private companies.

Investing means making precise choices, selecting one asset rather than another. If I invest in share ownership, it means that I am deducting money from the other 4 markets.

However, it should always be kept in mind that money is something unfaithful. Because if today it is aimed at a type of investment, tomorrow it will move towards another. So, if today precious metals are good, tomorrow will sooner or later go to the raw materials. For tomorrow, obviously, we mean after a few years. So, it's like a few years' engagements. But when he changes partners, he ends up betraying billions of people who believed in that area of investment. And every time it's a severe blow because the values collapse

History is full of such betrayals. In 2007, for example, it happened to properties and shares. And the latter collapsed in 2000 as well. In 1980, however, it was the turn of gold. Of course, the stories of love are also prolonged, like that of the stock market started in 1984 and came up to 2000. Or like the one started in 2000 up to 2007 on real estate.

Recently, however, money seems to have become attached to precious metals.

Therefore, money moves cyclically and even if it may happen that "fall in love" with more investment areas, it will do so more clearly towards an area. How to defend oneself from the volatility of the market? Surely inquire and train as much as possible, reading the economic news, taking a look at the countries on which to invest (considering their economic and political stability for example) or growing companies. Then it is advisable to rely on a trusted financial advisor to build your portfolio together.

What are the best assets to diversify your investments? Experts generally place MTB (acronym of multi-year Treasury Bonds) in the first place. Although the state coupons market is constantly evolving. In this historical moment, it is preferable to invest small amounts over the long term. However, it is worth stressing that these securities remain the safest investment to date, allowing a regular withdrawal of coupons with returns.

If we want faster and more substantial results, then the stock market is recommended for us. However, it must be said that large returns also correspond to much higher investment risks. So, we have to ponder perfectly how much to invest and on which institutions or companies. The properties are still to be avoided, since, after the bubble of the last decade, they have lost value. Although, it should also be added that the market believes that when the price falls, it is just the right time to buy. Just to get a regular monthly entry through rent. Or sell when the market is bullish again.

Bonds are another alternative, but it must be "guaranteed" and not subject to the performance of the companies to which they are affiliated. Finally, gold is always a good refuge, just like other precious materials or valuable paintings.

How to diversify our investments through the ETF? Many investors believe, naively, that it is enough to increase the number of investments to improve the diversification of the portfolio. But this is a dangerous simplification. If we invest our savings in individual securities, be they stocks or bonds, the number of products to be included in the portfolio must be raised to minimize the risk associated with each of the investments made.

On the other hand, if we invest our savings in active mutual funds or passive funds such as ETFs, we can achieve great diversification by reducing the number of instruments. Each fund (or ETF) is, in fact, a container of financial instruments, so with a few products, we can actually divide our portfolio into hundreds of different securities.

The main features of ETFs are:

- passive management
- their listing on the stock exchange as shares and bonds

With the former, it is intended that their return is closely linked to the listing of a stock exchange index and not to the fund manager's buying and selling ability. The stock index may be equity, commodity, bond, monetary, or other. The manager's job is limited to checking the consistency of the fund with the benchmark index. But also correct the value in the event of deviations. The difference between the price of the fund and that of the benchmark index is in the order of 1 or 2%.

"Passive management" therefore makes ETFs very cheap, to which is added their large or huge diversification, and their stock trading. All this makes them competitive compared to investing in individual stocks and less risky. However, there is also a lack of speculative lever leverage, inverted, or reversed leverage. ETFs are very convenient as they allow investing in many economic sectors: liquidity, bond indices, geographic equity markets, commodities, commodity sectors.

Example of diversification of investments

Suppose we have a capital to invest of 500 euros. And so, we decided to diversify investments in equal parts among the 5 assets. Now let's say that for each asset the trend was as follows:

Stocks: + 7%
Properties: - 6%
Commodities: - 10%
Precious metals: + 21%
Bonds: + 3%

Now, by making a calculation on the 100 euros invested per asset, we will have the following results: € 107 + € 94 + € 90 + € 121 + € 103 = € 515 total

We will, therefore, have earned € 15, or 3% on our initial invested capital. How is our result to be considered? It depends on our ambitions. If we play not to lose, then we will surely be satisfied. If we are traders who are content with little, we will be satisfied. If we do a more general calculation, perhaps considering an increase in personal expenses during the year, etc., then we will have a half reaction: we have not lost but not earned as well. If we are expert traders, then that 3% will appear miserable to us. Finally, if we are traders who want to push our earnings, then we will be completely dissatisfied. And we will think that perhaps having invested only in precious metals would have earned us 605 euros.

All this to say that the answer to the question of our satisfaction or not depends on us. From our ambitions. But of course, also from our formation. In fact, if we are beginners, then it is clear that for fear we will tend to distribute our money equally. But if we have the right experience and training on the subject, we will have the nose to invest in one or two assets only, those that we will consider being the winning ones.

Chapter 10: Swing Trading Options

Swing trading with options can be extremely difficult. This is why we decided to create this chapter, in which we go through some of the main ideas and concepts to always keep in mind, to be profitable from the start. Now, it is clear that at the beginning it is not easy to take money out of the market. However, with the right guidelines, it is not that difficult to achieve success in a short period of time. Anyway, let's get into some of the key factors to consider when it comes to swing trading with options.

- *"If you are undecided, stay still."* It is not necessary to invest continuously. If you do not have precise ideas, it is better to do nothing and wait for clearer signs. Often times, the market is full of indecision: keep calm and stack up money for the future.

- *"Cut losses and let profits run."* This is perhaps the best known and most important rule for those investing in the stock market. An indispensable factor for the application of this rule is the identification, immediately after the purchase, of the stop loss. This is how much you are willing to lose on that investment (consider when determining the average daily excursion of the stock). The cold and systematic application, even if painful, of the stop loss will preserve you from huge losses that would make the sale more and more traumatic, freezing capital that could be invested elsewhere.

- *"Learn from your mistakes."* Errors are not always negative: if you follow a strategy with a method, if you apply the stop losses, you will not make particularly serious mistakes. Errors are an integral part of stock trading: you need to analyze why you made them and what you can learn from them. In this way, a small loss can become a good investment lesson for the future.

- ***"Take profit and invest them back."*** If one of our titles is on the rise, take profit will be applied as the stock grows. A stock cannot grow indefinitely, when the trend is reversed, selling at the top, we will have had a profit avoiding further descents. If then the title should go up again, it does not matter, it will go better next time. You cannot always sell at the top since you cannot time the market.

- ***"Buy on the rumor and sell on the news."*** When positive news on a certain title officially comes out, pay attention. It may already be too late to invest in that title since the market could already have priced it in.

- ***Do not believe in "safe investments."*** If someone tells you that a title will certainly reach a certain price, he either does not understand much of the stock market or is only doing his own interests.

- ***"Never become emotionally attached to a stock."*** Some investors always follow a limited number of companies that they consider more reliable than others. There are no titles better than others, but only favorable situations and unfavorable situations. Often, instead of admitting an error, one perseveres on it with the consequence of being heavily unbalanced on a stock. This is really bad, especially if you are overcommitted to a stock in which, at that moment, the market does not believe in.

- ***"Always maintain certain liquidity available."*** Cyclically we find ourselves in situations of several days of generalized decline of the whole stock exchange and often, for lack of liquidity, we cannot grasp excellent buying opportunities. Keep some money aside to jump on big opportunities.

- ***"Choose the right platform."*** One important rule for investing in the stock market is that the platform makes a difference. Carefully selecting safe, honest and reliable trading platforms is the first step to make money. Those who start investing in the stock market for the first time must be careful to choose platforms that are really simple to use, perhaps with high-quality educational support. Some platforms also offer add-on tools, such as notifications, social trading and free analysis tools to guide less experienced traders.

- ***"Invest only in what you understand."*** As the "guru" of finance Warren Buffett said, "never, never, invest in something that you do not understand, and above all, that you do not know." The overwhelming majority of investors can achieve their capital growth goals by using the most common financial instruments, which are almost always simple to understand. The complex tools are best left to the great experts in the field.

- ***"Diversify your portfolio."*** When investing, the word to keep in mind is "diversification." Never invest in a single title, because if that sinks, your money will come to the same end. It is always better to have diversified investments to minimize the specific risks of a company, a market, an asset class or a currency. The more you diversify and the lower the probability of having drastic falls.

- ***"Understand and evaluate the risk."*** The risk is an intrinsic component of every investment. If it does not exist, there is no return. Whether they are government bonds, stocks or mutual funds, they all have a risk component, which will obviously be greater if you want to hope for higher returns. So, if someone tells you that there is an investment without risk, it means that it is better to get advice from someone else.

- ***"Look beyond direct investment."*** As an alternative to direct purchase of shares, it is possible to invest in the stock market indexes, through ETFs (listed mutual funds, which replicate the performance of equity and bond indices), or in mutual funds, that offer a high diversification even with minimum amounts, allow you to invest small periodic shares, for example 100 euros per month, and may even provide a monthly coupon.

- ***"Do not follow the masses."*** The typical decision of who buys stocks by investing in the stock market is usually strongly influenced by the advice of acquaintances, neighbors, or relatives. So, if everyone around is investing in a particular company, a beginner investor tends to do the same. But this strategy is bound to fail in the long run, and it is not the right approach. There should be no need to say that you should always avoid having a herd mentality if you do not want to lose hard-earned money on the stock market. The world's biggest investor, Warren Buffett, is right when he says, "Be fearful when others are greedy, and be greedy when others are fearful!"

- ***"Do not try to time the market."*** One thing that Warren Buffett does not do is try to time the stock market, even if he has a very strong understanding of the key price levels of the single shares. Most investors, however, do exactly the opposite, which often causes losses of money. So, you should never try to give timing to the market a chance. In reality, no one has ever succeeded in doing so successfully and consistently over multiple market cycles.

- ***"Be disciplined."*** Historically, it has often happened that during periods of a high market upswing, we first caused moments of panic. Market volatility has inevitably made investors poorer, even if the market moved in the intended direction. Therefore, it is prudent to have patience and follow a disciplined investment approach as well as keeping a long-term general picture in mind.

- ***"Be realistic and do not hope."*** There is nothing wrong with hoping to make the best investment, but you could be in trouble if the financial goals are not based on realistic assumptions. For example, many stocks have generated more than 50 percent of returns during the big uptrend in recent years. However, this does not mean that we can always expect the same kind of return from the stock exchange.

- ***"Keep your portfolio under control."*** We live in a connected world. Every important event that happens anywhere in the world also has an impact on our money. So, we have to monitor our portfolio and make adjustments constantly.

- ***"Be sure to be on the legal side of things."*** If someone proposes an investment, it must be verified as an "authorized project." In our country, those who offer financial investments must be authorized by law, and this is an important safeguard for savers. In fact, the authorization is issued only in the presence of the requested requisites and, once authorized, the financial intermediaries are subject to constant supervision. Checking this is not particularly demanding: if you have internet you can even directly access the information held by the supervisory authorities; otherwise you can contact the authorities themselves using traditional means.

- ***"Be skeptical and do your own research."*** Nobody gives anything for nothing: be wary of investment proposals that ensure a very high return. At the promise of high returns, there are usually very high risks or, in some cases, even attempts of fraud. Be wary of the "Ponzi schemes." These "operations," in fact, cannot guarantee any kind of return, as they are normally supplied exclusively by the continuity of the accessions. In other words, when the new signatures are no longer sufficient to pay the "interests" to the previous subscribers, the schemes are destined to fail. Be wary of the vague and generic investment proposals, for which the methods for using the money collected are not explained in detail (what kind of securities will be purchased, at what prices, on which markets, with which risk profiles - interest rate, foreign exchange or counterparty - and whether and which hedging instruments will be used to cover such risks).

- ***"Have a long-term mindset."*** According to Warren Buffett, the shares once bought, are not to be sold. It is, therefore, better to evaluate the industrial trends in the long term and then buy them, leaving aside the passengers' enthusiasm.

- ***"When investing in real estate, know the area you are investing in."*** To start with, it is good that you put your focus on your area of residence or, if you live in a big city, even on your neighborhood or on one that you know well. If you think to act on a field of action too large, you risk dispersing too much energy towards something that can present totally different solutions. Dedicate yourself only to residential buildings, apartments or houses. The commercial ones, even if they can be very profitable, have other rules and in general greater difficulties. The same for the land: you can do big business, but it is not something suitable for those who start.

- ***"Choose the right leverage and use it to your advantage."*** Real estate investments must be done with leverage. If you want to make an investment only with your money, then the essence of real estate investment is not clear to you. In fact, the concept of financial leverage allows you to invest with money that is not yours but to make money directly for you. Leverage an economic tool that allows you to get where you would not get only with your own strength. You can take out a mortgage (if you can afford it) or engage financial partners. It may seem strange to you, but it is not at all: even the richest need partners and remember that a figure that seems almost unimaginable to you, it may be normal to somebody else.

- ***"Verba volant, scripta manent"*** the Latins used to say. So never make verbal agreements, even if it is a relative or a childhood friend. Consult a lawyer to have the templates of the documents to be used. Like everything, at first it will seem difficult, but after a few times you will become an expert in basic legal practices for the sale of real estate, and you will be able to create documents in a very short time even by yourself.

- ***"Consider shorter positions."*** In the fixed income universe, a short duration approach is potentially able to reduce sensitivity to rising interest rates, while optimizing the returns/risk rations

- ***"Know your risk/reward ratio."*** A higher return may be tempting, but you must be sure not to take too many risks about the remuneration you would get. In bond markets, this means avoiding lengthening duration in a context of rising interest rates. Increasing investments in riskier assets may seem appropriate at the moment (when the macroeconomic scenario is quite positive), but it could turn out to be a rather risky choice if the situation should change. For example, the yields offered by high yield debt, on average 3% in Europe and 5.5% in the United States, would not be sufficient to compensate investors if insolvencies passed from their current level of 2% to a more normal one of the 5%. Conversely, market areas with a good risk/return profile, with high-rated issuers offering attractive returns, include emerging market debt, subordinated financial bonds, and hybrid corporate bonds. Aiming at long-term quality makes it possible to take on fair risks, helping to limit the impact of any negative macroeconomic event.

- *"Take the currency pairing into account."* Global investments are exposed to currency risks. High yield bonds and emerging market funds, for example, are usually denominated in US dollars, but the underlying bonds they hold may be issued in another currency. Fund managers may choose to include currency risk in the overall portfolio risk as exchange rates fluctuate or decide to contain this risk through currency hedging

- *"Stay flexible, keep some cash aside."* It is important to have the flexibility to underwrite and liquidate investments to seize the best opportunities. However, trades are expensive and can quickly erode earnings. This happens above all in the bond markets, given the relatively low levels of returns. The bid-ask spread is on average 30-40% of the yield, so an excess of trades erodes this margin and obviously reduces the total return.

Even holding portfolios with structurally short duration, allowing short-term bonds to come to maturity naturally, can improve returns because you will effectively pay the bid-ask spread once.

- **"Build up your portfolio over time."** If investing a small sum such as 5000 Euro, will not allow you to live on that income, it can certainly represent an opportunity, to make money. Also, even if you have good economic availability, the ideal is always "to make it safe," start to invest from small figures and then fuel the investment over time.

- **"The past does not equal the future."** The story is not indicative of how an investment will result in the future and investors should always try to weigh the potential risks associated with a particular investment, as well as its possible returns.

Once you have established a profitable options trading strategy that generates a passive income every single month, you cannot fly to Thailand and live the laptop lifestyle just yet. As the millionaire Tony Robbins said, *just because it works, it does not mean it will last forever*. I really want this to sink in as it is one of the most important notions of the entire book.

When things are moving in the right direction, it is time to triple down on your effort and truly commit yourself to mastery. In particular, there is one thing that I'd like you to do once the first profits start to come.

Find a mentor

One of the great things about success is that it leaves footsteps: almost anything you would like to do to improve your life has already been done by someone else. It does not matter whether you are starting a business, beginning your trading journey, having a happy marriage, losing weight, quitting smoking, running a marathon or simply organizing a perfect lunch. There is certainly someone who did it very well and has left some clues.

When you are able to take advantage of these precious clues, you will discover that life is like a game in which you must connect the dots, and all the dots have already been identified and organized by others. All you have to do is follow their project and use their system.

Chapter 11: Things to Ponder Before Entering the Market

In this chapter, we will go deep into the subject and discover the 15 golden lessons that every investor should know, before entering the stock market.

Easy Money is Like Santa Claus: "It does not exist!"

One who promises to quintuple your assets without sweating is not more than a seller of smoke. Investing in the stock market is not a joke. To achieve the investment goals, you have set yourself to avoid risky securities, focus on something more stable, lasting, and profitable. In the recipe for success, in addition to a serious knowledge of the stock markets, there is also the sentimental component (for those investing there is no room for panic but a lot of patience) and even a bit of luck.

Gold and Cash do not Give Interest

Everyone knows that cash does not disappear, but after the bizarre maneuvers of the European Central Bank (which brought negative returns on the single currency), we can be even more certain that investing in cash does not create any interest. The dream of all is to be able to accumulate that amount of money enough to enjoy a quiet retirement but the closer it gets to the time x, the more the small investor tends to panic. Hence the reckless choices to invest in cash or in commodities such as gold which, although it proves to be more stable than fiat, cannot hold the same value forever. Just think that in the last luster, the value of the most precious metal fell by 34.8%.

The Recipe for a Winning Strategy

One of the main factors of success on the stock exchange is sentiment: patience, foresight, and prudence are the three basic ingredients of winning strategies, but it is also true that a little risk never hurts.

If the money we have invested on a certain stock does not return, you should look around and find some slightly riskier but at least profitable activity, with the hope that an important injection of money into the markets can restart the economy by stimulating productivity and development.

Establish Investment Goals

Before starting to invest, then embark on a challenging and long path, you must have clear in mind where you want to go. It depends on personal aspirations, on the trust that one has for himself and on many other factors. However, the main choice is between protecting capital and making it grow. Under certain conditions, the stock exchange also lends itself to the speculative approach. Who wants to start could also establish concrete objectives such as buying a good or a service. In any case, the rule is always the same: to understand where you want to arrive.

Establish the Degree of Risk Tolerance

This is probably the most important phase. The stock market is in fact extremely varied and allows numerous approaches, from the prudent and static to the dynamic and courageous.

This is why it is always good to establish one's degree of tolerance. Based on this decision, further choices will be made, until the real investment is realized. Investor profiles depend on personal characteristics and their economic situation. If you are a simple worker, do not sail in gold and maybe those who invest are the savings of a lifetime, it is good to give up any speculative ambitions. The degree of tolerance determines the risk that you intend to run and the strategy that will be adopted later.

Studying

The information issue should not be forgotten. The stock market is complex, structurally risky, so we need to be cautious. The risk is to lose capital in a short period. Therefore, it is necessary to undertake a training course that confers at least the theoretical tools. The topic of the study should consist of both the investment modalities - how it is invested in the concrete - and the economic environment in general.

As for the sources, including paper texts, successful books, and the internet, you are spoiled
with choices.

The study activity, however, never abandons the investor, even when he has become an expert. Pressing is the need to update continuously, but also to inquire about everything that gravitates around the securities in the portfolio.

Choose the Long Term

Investing in the stock market should not be an activity of a few months or even a few years. It must be a continuous activity. It is only through patience and perseverance that it is possible to make substantial profits. This means that you need to build a long-term version (which looks at least for the next five years [ten is more suitable]). This means that it is okay not to give in to the temptation to sell the securities as soon as the prices start to fall. Life is worth the saying, "laugh well who laughs last."

Monitoring

If you opt for a long-term vision, as you should, then it is essential to monitor the status of your investment. Not everyone knows that control and monitoring begin before the investment itself. In particular, it is necessary to establish a benchmark, i.e., a yardstick by means of which it is possible to really understand whether we are on the right path or not. Finally, it is good to make a periodic comparison between the expected results and the real ones. In the beginning, there is a strong temptation to abandon oneself to discouragement, also because the results tend to arrive farther with time.

A general consideration can be made on the segment within which to operate. In fact, everything depends on risk tolerance. If this is very low, you should address those segments that by their nature do not suffer from the crisis. The reference is to those goods whose consumption is practically mandatory, therefore the food and pharmaceuticals. Investing in pharmaceutical companies' actions will not make you rich but is a very useful asset to protect capital. Strangely enough, but up to a certain point, the high-tech segment (e.g., mobile phones, social networks, etc.) also plays a similar role.

Investing in the stock market can be a business that can increase its capital. In addition to technical knowledge, we need some moral skills: patience, perseverance, lucidity, foresight. All qualities that must be cultivated and that can make the difference. Vice versa will never give good fruits an approach based on imprudence, on haste, from the frenzy of profit.

Use the Leverage

What unfortunately many traders do not consider is investing in the stock market or trading online using leverage. To invest in the stock market with little money, it is necessary to deepen the study of this tool, which will allow us to expose our capital to a huge risk. We recommend the use of leverage only on a reduced capital, carried out concurrently also with a rationalized use of stop loss and take profit. Besides, you must always have your budget under control using careful Money Management. Finally, before investing in the stock market, you need to study the markets and all the financial instruments on which you want to invest in.

"You do not need to be a finance guru to invest in the stock market!"

Obviously, we are not telling you that the market should not be studied or that there must be a basis for training. One who applies himself and follows the markets, deepening the subject, will always know more than others.

So, we always recommend following the training path of your broker, which will allow you not to take missteps throughout the investment process. Through taking advantage of the online trading demo platforms, it is possible to simulate the investment and understand where mistakes are made and avoid them when investing with a real account.

Conclusion

Thank you and congratulations for making it through to the end of *"Options Trading."* Let's hope that it was informative and able to provide you with all of the tools you need to achieve your financial goals.

The next step is to begin applying what you have learned during this book. Our suggestion is always to open up a demo account on a broker and make a few tries before putting real money into it. Remember that you should never risk more than what you can afford to lose; so manage your capital wisely.

We hope that you find these lessons valuable and that you got the information you were looking for. Letting your money work for you will give you an incredible feeling, especially at the beginning when you make the first gains. We are thrilled for you to start, and we cannot wait to see your results coming in!